Heroes or Traitors

The German Replacement Army,
the July Plot, and Adolf Hitler

WALTER S. DUNN, JR.

Westport, Connecticut
London

ISBN: 0–275–97715–3

Praeger Publishers, 88 Post Road West, Westport, CT 06881
An imprint of Greenwood Publishing Group, Inc.

Printed in the United States of America

Contents

Preface

Twenty years after the publication of my book on the second front, many historians still believe the cover story promulgated during the Second World War that the American army was unprepared to fight after three years of preparation that had begun in June 1940. Implicit in this interpretation is the notion that Gen. George C. Marshall was foolhardy in his insistence that the American divisions were ready. Also implied is that Americans were rather deficient as soldiers if they could not be trained sooner. Neither was the case.

The Second World War was a political matter conducted by three very astute politicians on the Allied side and an equally astute Adolf Hitler controlling Germany. The outcome of major events was more often determined by the political ramifications than by military strength. Resources were squandered on pointless campaigns such as Italy and Burma, which had no strategic objective but did have post-war political significance. While these sideshows were staged, campaigns of immense strategic importance were delayed or canceled for lack of resources.

The primary objective of the German generals who conspired to remove Hitler, take over Germany, and negotiate an early end to the war in July 1944 was to have Germany emerge intact from the war and ready to join an alliance against the Soviet Union. This prospect was not as unreasonable as may appear when one considers the alignment of nations that was to emerge during the Cold War. Both Winston Churchill and Franklin D. Roosevelt believed that they had no need for a strong Germany to balance the power of the Soviet Union, and they would have rejected any such offer. However, they were definitely interested in ending the war as soon as possible, to reduce the loss of life. That goal in fact was achieved as an indirect result of the actions of the conspirators, as this work will describe.

This book is the product of more than sixty years of study, beginning with an avid interest in the events of the Second World War as it was being fought. Undergraduate work at Durham University in England under Dr. H.C. Offler drilled home the philosophy that one must study the details before making sweeping generalizations. Among my professors at Durham was Professor Eric Birley, who headed the British order-of-battle intelligence organization during the war and whose name pops up as attending various planning sessions, with little description of his role.

Orders of battle, logistics, and training—not fascinating topics to nonspecialists—seldom appear in popular histories. However, those matters often reveal the true situations and options available. This book includes a considerable amount of detail concerning these topics.

I have had personal experience with two of the main themes of this work, the use of military force to maintain order in a city and the rapid organization of military units. In the summer of 1942, the city of Detroit was paralyzed by a race riot that brought war production almost to a halt. A half-mile from my home, a group of some twenty men with baseball bats, shotguns, and rifles gathered at one of the major east-west streets and stopped automobiles driven by blacks who were returning from work on the west side of Detroit to the black neighborhood on the east side. Other streets were blocked by similar gangs. In reaction to that violent move, black gangs destroyed the white-owned businesses in the black neighborhoods. Overwhelmed and unable to cope with the large crowds, the Detroit police needed assistance.

The army sent 3,000 men of the 38th Infantry Regiment to Detroit to restore order. One battalion was bivouacked on the Detroit Public Library lawn a half-mile from my home, and another battalion was on the athletic field of Northwestern High School, where my older sister was a student. Order was instantly restored; both whites and blacks hesitated to confront the heavily armed soldiers. As I was told by men who had been in the regiment in 1942, their orders were firm—the riot had disrupted war production and was aiding the enemy.

Four years later I was myself assigned to the 38th Infantry Regiment, which in the spring of 1946 was being reconstituted. As a young soldier with a high classification-test score, I was made the administrative assistant to the personnel officer of the regiment. During the next few months I worked long hours as the regiment absorbed over 3,000 recruits, reenlisted veterans, and over a hundred officers who had returned to service after being separated in 1945.

My responsibility was completing the paperwork allocating officers to the eighteen companies and five batteries in the regimental combat team, consisting of the infantry regiment, an artillery battalion, a medical company, and an engineer company. The combat team included several light-plane pilots in the artillery battalion. Because all officers not promoted for a stated time were automatically promoted one grade when separated, the regiment included only one second lieutenant, a recent graduate of West Point. Most companies had two captains and four first lieutenants.

Within two months the regiment was completely functional. Men had been trained in the use of heavy weapons; the antitank and cannon companies, both equipped with tanks, were operational; and the regiment had embarked on advanced training as a mountain infantry regiment under the guidance of veterans of the 10th Mountain Division.

Not to place too much emphasis on personal experience, one does gather impressions that clarifies information in written records. Moving a troop train with more than 400 men nearly 2,000 miles from New Jersey to Colorado in four days was a common occurrence in 1946, despite the fact that the higher priority of passenger and freight trains forced troop trains to spend many hours on sidings awaiting their turns to use the track. In contrast, moving a train 400 miles from Germany to Paris (a trip that I made in 1948) with top priority was an overnight event in 1944.

Most of the factual data presented in the book is documented in the sources listed in the bibliography. The remainder have come from my personal files of unit histories that have accumulated over many years.

Any work of this nature is the product of many hands. My wife has been foremost in her patient editing of drafts and suggestions for clarification of obscure points. As willing listeners, Tom Johnson and David McNamara have offered insights on the German army and its order of battle. The help of the staff of the University of Wisconsin Library in locating sources was given without stint. During my several visits to the home of Gen. Albert C. Wedemeyer, he provided behind-the-scenes details concerning the negotiations in 1943 that led to the postponement of the second front in France. The contributions of these individuals and many others were invaluable.

Introduction

Every spring after 1939, the Germans organized large batches of divisions for the summer campaign. Then suddenly in January 1944 this routine was stopped. In other words, the organization of new divisions was their usual practice every spring until the spring of 1944, when the need was the most urgent. Errors of omission are often more damaging than errors of commission. More difficult to detect, errors of omission often escape the notice of those who could correct the fault.

The purpose of this book is to establish that errors of omission did take place. One of the major oversights for which I have no "smoking gun" was a directive ordering the Replacement Army to halt the release of troops to the field army at a critical time. I have only a statistical indication that more than 600,000 German troops did not move from the Replacement Army to the field army between February and July 1944. With the release of these troops, the formation of at least sixty new divisions would have been possible before June 1944, as would have been the maintenance of the combat effectiveness of the divisions under attack in France and Russia in June and July.

To establish the fact that a serious error of omission was committed, the book describes the circumstances that could have been expected had the errors not been made. Given the past performance of the German army on the Russian front, the German army with proper replacements could have been more successful.

The Russian front in World War II became a bloodbath of gigantic proportions. Germany and her allies lost about four million killed during the war; Soviet military casualties were more than double that number. With this steady drain of killed, wounded, and missing, both Germany and the Soviet Union developed sophisticated systems that churned out millions of replacements every year. The Russians were able to maintain about six million on the German front and an additional five million on other fronts and behind the lines. The Germans reached a peak of twelve million men on all fronts in 1944. While the Germans had 3.1 million on the Russian front in July 1943, by February 1944 the total had dropped to 2.4 million, as the flow of new divisions and replacements was cut. After February 1944 only a minimum flow of replacements went to the front, and few new divisions were formed.

Since 1941 the existence of a powerful strategic reserve of fresh divisions had proved to be essential to both offensive and defensive battles in the East. These fresh divisions were added to sectors in order to provide the Germans with either local superiority for an offensive or the means to stop a Soviet offensive.

France was the training ground for the German strategic reserve beginning in June 1941. The availability of new or rebuilt divisions almost every six months gave the German high command a strong hand in determining the activity on the eastern front. After November 1943, with the Allied invasion of France impending, no further divisions from France were available for the East, depriving the Germans of the strategic initiative.

The lack of a strategic reserve in June 1944 was a direct result of preparations for the coup of July 1944. At great risk to their own lives, the plotters intended to end the war quickly, as Germany obviously could not win. The primary objective was not to kill Hitler or take over the government but to end the war. The attempt to kill Hitler was only a necessary first step. These steps, undertaken with great reluctance, were required to begin negotiations with the Western Allies.

The plot that culminated on 20 July 1944 had two components: the attempted assassination of Adolf Hitler, and the subsequent attempt to take over the government of Germany. The conspirators believed correctly that if the military coup were to succeed, the removal of Hitler was essential, because the western Allies would not negotiate with him.

As long as Hitler lived, overthrowing the Nazi rule would be difficult. Each soldier had sworn allegiance to him personally, and Hitler had to be removed to relieve the army of its oath. The first message to the public by the conspirators was to have been that Hitler had been killed by members of the Nazi Party and that the military takeover was intended to rid the nation of the traitors who had killed the Führer.

Hitler also had to be killed because of the extraordinary confidence of the German people in their leader. Hitler, despite his reprehensible policies, had the support of the overwhelming majority of Germans. Even after his death, the German public was likely not to renounce him or his policies. Without the support of the majority of the people, the generals would need a large military force within hours to control the country after the assassination. The generals believed, with some justification, that they would need the Replacement Army to take control of the government and suppress any possible rising.

In the event, believing that Hitler was dead, the plotters issued as their first orders an alert to troops in the Replacement Army to take control of the cities and towns. The Gross Deutschland Replacement Brigade did come to Berlin and took control of many government offices.

The Replacement Army had to provide the troops for civilian control; therefore the conspirators planned that trained men be held there. To ensure that enough troops were available throughout Germany to take control and to prevent any civil uprising or difficulty with the SS, it was absolutely necessary to withhold replacements for the field army. That this was done was ample evidence of the plotters' awareness that they did not have the support of the people.

For this purpose, the generals held over a half-million men in Germany, men who should have been at the front. For the sake of secrecy, men were retained in the Replacement Army without the knowledge of many of the conspirators. Very likely only a few of the conspirators were aware that troops were being deliberately withheld from the front; the effect was spread across more than 700 replacement battalions in Germany. Delaying the dispatch of a single battalion of a thousand men either to the front as replacements, or to a new division, was not a noteworthy event, especially as the existing divisions were at full strength on 1 June 1944.

Only a few of the conspirators in staff positions of the Replacement Army were aware of the total picture. Hitler was completely unaware, as indicated by his concern over the upgrading of two *Landesschutzen* (home guard) divisions to combat status by the replacement of older men with new recruits. This relatively insignificant action was the topic of the fatal meeting on 20 July 1944.

Although the conspirators failed to kill Hitler or take over the government, they did achieve the ultimate goal: they were successful in shortening the war, if at the expense of their own lives. The German catastrophes that occurred in the East and the West and hastened the end were direct results of the lack of reserve divisions and replacements.

Another factor that facilitated halting the creation of new divisions in February 1944 was the fact that Hitler, who previously had reviewed every detail of the war, became increasingly ill. There is considerable evidence that Hitler was suffering from Parkinson's disease and that the symptoms were becoming worse in 1944. Although the disease did not incapacitate Hitler mentally, tremors and the lack of muscular control must have impeded his ability to manage the many details involved in directing the war. He may also have suffered from other conditions that impaired his mental capacity. Because Hitler refused treatment, the symptoms became notably worse in 1944 and apparently decreased his ability to direct affairs—even more to the advantage of the conspirators in their effort to conceal their management of the Replacement Army.

From June 1941 to November 1943, when Hitler was in full control, divisions had been assembled and trained in France. Creating divisions began with assembling cadres, shipping in recruits, and training both the new men and the divisions as a whole. One group of new divisions, replacing those lost at Stalingrad, was sent to Italy, where it halted the Allies. Four groups went to the East between 1942 and 1943, providing the impetus for new offensives. From November 1943 to June 1944, thirty-seven divisions were formed or rebuilt to oppose the second front in June 1944. Each group of divisions played a major role in the events from the winter of 1941–1942, when a group helped reestablish the front after the Soviet winter offensive, until the fall of 1943.

Gen. Erich von Manstein, commander of Army Group South, launched his counteroffensive in the Spring of 1943 with divisions transferred from France. In the summer of 1943, a fresh group of divisions gave the Germans the means to launch the Kursk offensive. After its failure to break through at Kursk, the German army retreated in the face of multiple Soviet operations. Finally, in October 1943, with the arrival of a fresh group of German divisions from France, the Russians were stopped at Kiev.

Hitler's edict of 3 November 1943, to increase the effort to create new divisions in the West to oppose the second front that was expected in May 1944, and to send no additional divisions from France to the Russian front, was the result of the meeting of the Allied leaders in Yalta in late 1943 and their agreement to launch a second front in 1944. On the same day as the edict, the Soviets launched the attack that took Kiev and broke the German defense line in the Ukraine. Faced with the need to send cadres for new divisions to France while trying to stem the Soviet advance, the Germans formed corps detachments in the East, division-sized units made up of the remnants of two or three divisions. These makeshift divisions helped the Germans once again stabilize the Russian front.

The Russians were comparatively quiet for the first six months of 1944, at least in the north and center. From January to June 1944, there was little movement in the East, allowing the Germans to rebuild their divisions in the north and center merely with returning wounded. The buildup in the West also proceeded on schedule, improving existing divisions and using cadres from the East to rebuild burned-out divisions. A force of more than fifty divisions was created to oppose the invasion.

However, these efforts were far from adequate; while the overall strength of the German field army increased slightly, the bulk of the new soldiers were held in the Replacement Army. In June 1944 simultaneous assaults in Normandy and on Army Group Center caused more losses to the Germans in June and July than in any other two months during the war. Whereas in the past the Germans had been able to transfer divisions from France to seal gaps in the East, they could not do so in June 1944. The Replacement Army refused to create "alarm units," created by assembling units from the Replacement

Army into combat formations, and send them to the front in these months, even though 400 combat replacement battalions, equal to nearly sixty divisions, were available in the Replacement Army in Germany.

They were not sent to the front because the generals plotting to kill Hitler in July 1944 planned to use the Replacement Army instead to cope with possible civil unrest in Germany following Hitler's assassination. Rather than being assembled into divisions and regimental groups to cope with the emergency, as in the past, trained men were held in the replacement battalions throughout Germany.

Neither the East nor West had enough forces to withstand the attacks once the offensives began in June 1944. In August, after the assassination failed, the flow of men resumed. However, until September few additional forces arrived at the fronts from Germany. Although these new divisions enabled the Germans to stabilize the situation on both fronts in the fall of 1944, the effect of the lack of reserve divisions in the East and West in June 1944 was that the offensive was not stopped until the Red Army had reached the Vistula River and the western Allies reached the Rhine.

The Replacement Army in the spring of 1944 delayed the formation of new divisions that Hitler certainly would have promptly sent to the front. Instead, it concealed about 600,000 men in a variety of noncombat units, including *Schatten* (shadow) divisions formed to rebuild battle-worn divisions in the future.

The lack of 600,000 men on the western and eastern fronts played a significant role in the disasters of June and July 1944. Had these men been available, the sixty new German infantry divisions that could have been formed between January and April 1944 would have made a difference. Instead, in the five months from February to June 1944 the Replacement Army created only four *Schatten* divisions and five occupation divisions.

After the coup failed to kill Hitler and the plotters were eliminated from their command positions, a massive number of new divisions were created in a few short months from the ample supply of manpower previously held back. In late July and August, with Hitler back in control, the Replacement Army created forty-eight infantry divisions and nine *Schatten* divisions in six weeks. The culmination of this rebuilding effort was the assembly of two panzer armies in the Ardennes that dealt the Americans a stunning blow in December 1944.

Not only did the Replacement Army fail to form new divisions prior to June 1944, it also failed to provide individual replacements for divisions in combat once the heavy fighting commenced in June 1944. The Replacement Army delayed the dispatch of urgently needed reinforcements to both the eastern and western fronts. Only 10,000 replacements were sent to Normandy in the first six weeks of fighting to offset 110,000 losses. Without replacements in the rifle companies, the infantry divisions lost their combat effectiveness and were reduced to battle groups.

The lack of replacements and of the additional divisions that should have been formed had a serious impact on the conduct of the battles in both the East and West. The result was the loss of over 800,000 Germans reported killed and missing in July and August 1944, compared to a usual monthly loss of 100,000 men in those categories. In view of the rapid rebuilding of the German army in August of 1944 after the conspirators had been removed, there is little question that replacements had been available and that additional divisions could have been formed earlier. These omissions culminated in an earlier end of the war in Europe, to the benefit of all countries involved.

Catastrophic German losses in France and White Russia in the summer of 1944 were the direct result of lack of reserves. Given these enormous losses, the assumption would be that the Allies and the Soviet Union would continue to march on Berlin, but once Hitler had removed the conspirators he was able to release the troops and weapons for the front and to restore the situation by October 1944. However, because 800,000 men had been lost in the summer, the end came in 1945, and few battles of the intensity of Stalingrad were fought on German soil.

The catastrophes in July and August 1944 were not mere coincidences. One should consider the mathematical probabilities and then look for some cause-and-effect relationship. That the German army suffered more losses, primarily prisoners, in July and August of 1944 than in any other two months of the war and miraculously restored its strength in September can be explained neither as a coincidence nor as a fortuitous combination of circumstances.

The ability of Germany to cope with large-scale offensives on several fronts in Russia had been proven time and again. If the combined forces of the British, Americans, and Russians had reached such a level in July and August that German resistance was ineffective, leading to the debacles that occurred in both East and West, why was the German army able to contain both fronts in September, even though the opposing armies were growing steadily in strength? The Allied and Soviet armies continued to advance in the following eight months, but they did so at enormous cost to themselves and at comparatively low cost to the Germans.

The reason for the momentary failure of the German army in the late summer of 1944 was lack of the usual flow of new units, replacements, and new equipment to the fronts from Germany. Instead of maintaining the steady flow of men and material to the front, the flow was abruptly halted at a time when troops and weapons were sorely needed on both fronts. By August 1944 even the handful of divisions that were transferred from other army groups were able to halt the Soviet offensive in White Russia. Only a few German divisions were able to halt the drive of Gen. George S. Patton, Jr., in September (Patton claimed to have logistical problems). Had the units held back in Germany been formed into divisions, as was the established practice, and sent to the front in June and July, they might well have been enough to reduce the scale of German losses and prolong the war for many months. Hitler himself commented after the plotters had finally been eradicated that once again the troops and equipment were flowing to the fronts.

In retrospect, both the Allies and the German people benefited greatly from the conspiracy. Because the war was shortened, hundreds of thousands of Germans were made prisoners rather than losing their lives in pointless, desperate battles, and, of course, the lives of many Allied troops were saved. Tens of thousands of inmates were rescued from concentration camps who could not have endured another year.

Germany was saved the pain of an additional year of air bombardment and the possible use of the atomic bomb had American casualties in Europe continued at a high rate. The bombing of Dresden in the final days of the war was an example of what could have happened to many cities in Germany had the war gone on. Few German cities in the West were subjected to the ferocious battles of the kind that destroyed Stalingrad, Berlin, and other cities that had been declared "fortresses" by Hitler.

The Allies were spared the hundreds of thousands of killed and wounded that would have resulted from a last-ditch defense by a

German army still intact and fighting for every foot of ground in France and White Russia, and later in Germany.

Therefore the world has to appreciate the conspirators' achievement, at the cost of their lives, even though the scenario that developed was not what they had envisioned.

The Replacement Army

The German replacement system in World War II was based on the experience of World War I, when infantry divisions required a steady stream of new men to replace the casualties in the crushing toll of trench warfare. Four years of bitter trench warfare caused a steady drain of killed, wounded, and missing in all of the armies engaged on the Western Front. To cope with the never-ending demand for replacements, Germany created an elaborate system of replacement and training battalions throughout the country. Each German division was linked to a particular town and province; replacement battalions provided replacements for specific divisions from the same district.

This system was re-created in World War II. As each infantry regiment entered active service in 1939, it left behind elements that formed a replacement battalion. However, fighting in World War II was quite different from World War I; casualties were much fewer. From September 1939 until June 1941 Germany experienced only trivial casualties in fewer than three months of heavy combat in all three campaigns—Poland, France, and the Balkans. Even so, the Replacement Army continued to induct and train a steady flow of men. The limited losses of the first two years of World War II left a surplus of replacements. With this excess manpower the Germans were able to create additional divisions. In the spring of 1941, in preparation for Germany's invasion of Russia, many new divisions were created from both newly trained men and cadres taken from existing divisions. With the increasing number of divisions, replacement battalions became responsible for providing men for entire divisions rather than regiments.

More than 700 replacement and training battalions were formed in Germany during World War II. Each replacement battalion included companies that gave basic training to recruits, as well as companies that provided advanced training and others rehabilitated men returned from hospitals. At any given time there would be varying numbers of companies of each type and a wide range of company strengths. Because the flow of men from hospitals varied greatly and the number of inductees in the training companies varied as well, it was simple to conceal the presence of large numbers of trained men in the Replacement Army. Only a battalion-by-battalion study of the daily returns would reveal the total. Even then the subjective judgment of the commander of the replacement battalion determined how many men were fit for duty and ready for combat. One German veteran whom I interviewed had had prior military service before his induction in World War II. After four days in a replacement battalion, including one day at the rifle range to test his skill, he was declared ready for duty and sent to a battalion in France.

The time recuperating wounded men spent assigned to a replacement battalion varied according to the severity of the wound. The recuperating soldiers were assigned to various duties, including *Landesschutzen* battalions guarding prisoners. The new inductees required very little basic training, compared to the American army. Young Germans entering the army were already familiar, from their period in the Hitler Youth, with rifles, machine pistols, and other small arms, which they had fired on ranges under the direction of skilled instructors. Physical training was provided as well. The plan was to give the young men combat simulation exercises in the advanced training companies. Also, older men and ethnic Germans drafted from areas occupied by the German army usually had previous military training. Advanced combat training was not essential for a rifleman who would spend his first months at the front in a divisional field replacement battalion, which gave him combat training under seasoned veterans. The cadre of the divisional replacement battalion decided when a recruit was ready for assignment to a rifle company.

New recruits received from three to eight weeks of basic training, depending on the judgment of the company officers as to when the men were ready. After the men finished basic training, a small percentage, usually those destined for the Russian front, were sent for advanced training. Others went for a few weeks of specialist training as heavy howitzer gunners, panzer grenadiers, or reconnaissance troops. At a camp at Küstrin, two men who had been reservists in the Polish army were given only three weeks of training before being sent to Africa.

The organization of the replacement battalions and divisions changed in 1942, when the replacement training battalions were split into a training battalion and a replacement battalion. Replacement and training battalions normally consisted of three rifle companies and one machine-gun training company, as well as one or more convalescent companies and one or more "march" or temporary companies to transfer men to the front. When the split of the replacement and training battalions occurred, the staff of the original battalion usually became the staff of the new training battalion. A new staff was created for the replacement battalion, and new companies were formed to provide basic training to the incoming soldiers, while the existing companies became part of the new training battalions, which provided advanced training.

Later, some of the training battalions were redesignated reserve battalions and formed into regiments and reserve divisions that performed occupation duty in France, the Soviet Union, and other occupied territory. The reserve divisions were an outgrowth of the replacement division commands in each military district and received men from battalions in their parent districts. Usually the staff of the replacement division assumed the command of the reserve division, and a new replacement division staff was created in the military district. The reserve division would include the training battalions formed from the replacement battalions in the district previously under the command of the replacement division.

The system can best be described by using the example of a man born in 1925 and inducted into the army in January 1943 at the reception company of the 588th Replacement Battalion in Hannover, in Military District XI. In January he was sent with nine other recruits to a camp in Nijmegen, the Netherlands, for basic training. In February 1943 he was sent to a training company in the 211th Reserve Infantry Battalion in the 171st Reserve Division in Culenborg, the Netherlands. After three months he completed his training, and in

April he was sent to a march company of the 211th Replacement Battalion in Hanover. In June the march company was sent to the 895th Infantry Regiment of the 265th Infantry Division, which was being formed in Hameln, in Military District XI. Because he had joined a newly forming division, his home replacement battalion became the 12th Infantry Replacement Battalion at Halberstadt, which was to provide replacements for the new 265th Infantry Division. He was assigned to the 6th Company of the 895th Grenadier Regiment of the 265th Division.

The reserve divisions remained a part of the Replacement Army, which was organized according to the twenty-one military districts in Germany and also had units in the General Government in Poland and in the Bohemia-Moravia district in Czechoslovakia. In 1941 there were 1.4 million men in the Replacement Army, including a million men engaged in training and 200,000 recuperating wounded. Conditions changed during the winter of 1941, when the grinding battles of attrition in the USSR increased the demand for men to the very high World War I levels. By then, as noted above, the German replacement system had been altered by the new divisions: instead of a replacement battalion providing men for only a regiment, the battalions were supporting entire divisions. Nevertheless the system was effective in 1942, as the Germans rebuilt battered divisions in France and created additional ones from newly trained men and cadres of old divisions.

Each soldier retained an affiliation with his original replacement battalion unless he was transferred to another division, in which case his replacement battalion was changed to reflect his new assignment. Sometimes the assignment of a replacement battalion would change, especially during the transition from serving regiments to serving divisions. The 125th Frontier Infantry Replacement Battalion in Saarbrucken, in Military District XI, had originally provided replacements for the 125th Frontier Regiment. In 1941 the regiment was assigned to the 164th Division, which was later motorized and sent to Africa as part of the Afrika Korps. The 125th Motorized Infantry Regiment thereafter received replacements from the battalion that served the 164th Division. The 125th Replacement Battalion was then assigned to provide replacements for the new 65th Division in France.

The importance of the affiliation with a certain replacement battalion was that when a soldier was wounded or became ill, he returned to the same battalion. In the example above, the soldier was affiliated with a replacement battalion in Military District XI, despite many changes in assignment, until his transfer to the 65th Division.

To explain the system for handling wounded soldiers, we can use the example of a veteran born in 1917 and inducted in 1938. In 1941 he was a member of the 76th Motorized Artillery Regiment of the 6th Panzer Division in Russia. He was wounded near Poltava in August 1943, contracted jaundice, and was cared for in several field hospitals, as well as in a reserve hospital in Poland and a hospital in Vienna. The hospital in Vienna informed his replacement battalion, the 1st Battalion of the 76th Motorized Artillery Replacement Regiment in Wuppertal, in Military District VI; the battalion then assigned him to the convalescent battery of the battalion, even though he remained in a Vienna hospital. When he was well enough to perform limited service, he was sent to the 217th *Landesschutzen* Battalion at Geldern, in Military District VI, to guard prisoners of war. When he was fully recovered, he returned to the 1st Battalion of the 76th Artillery Replacement Regiment and, after passing through the reception company, was assigned to a march company. Later, after attending a noncommissioned officer training school at Krefeld and receiving a short furlough, he was sent to the 16th Motorized Artillery Regiment of the 16th Panzer Division, a Stalingrad division being reformed in France. The 1st Battalion of the 76th Artillery Replacement Regiment provided replacements for the artillery regiments of both the 6th and 16th Panzer Divisions, because the 16th Panzer Division had been formed from elements of the 6th Panzer in 1941. Therefore, as the need in the 16th Panzer was greater, our veteran was sent there rather than being returned to his original division as would have been usual.

From these examples, one can see the key role of the replacement battalion in the flow of manpower in the German army. In contrast, the American army sent men from all around the United States to replacement training companies and, after training was completed, sent them to replacement centers like Camp Kilmer, New Jersey. There they were arbitrarily formed into replacement companies and sent overseas to replacement depots, where they were assigned to units as needed. In the German system, the recruit would remain in the company of men from his own home area with whom he had trained; American recruits, in contrast, were deliberately denied the morale-boosting camaraderie of familiar faces, to prevent shock to a community if a unit were captured or suffered heavy losses of men all from the same area. I can remember well the distress in Detroit in 1942 when the casualties were listed for a Canadian battalion from Windsor, Ontario, that had been at Dieppe. Windsor is just across the Detroit River, and many men from Detroit had enlisted in the battalion. An American recruit seldom met a man with whom he had trained. I myself met only one, a former cadre man in my training company who was assigned to me six months later as an assistant—a remarkable twist of fate.

While the German system helped maintain unit integrity, it was cumbersome, and in the summer of 1944 it allowed German generals countless opportunities to delay secretly the transfer of men from the Replacement Army to the front, especially by delaying the documentation of march companies and march battalions, though they were actually in existence. Falsified reports listed the men as still in the convalescent and training companies.

The German practice was to maintain the frontline rifle company strength at about 100 men, despite the official tables of organization. This number was adequate to operate the heavy weapons, machine guns, mortars, and rocket launchers assigned to the company. The heavy weapons provided the company with firepower, whereas additional riflemen were of little value, other than as replacements for the heavy-weapons crews. Therefore, new men were held behind the lines in the field training battalion and released to the rifle companies only as needed to replace casualties. However, if the flow from the Replacement Army was cut off, as the shrewd commanders in the replacement system managed to do, the field training battalions would be rapidly drained of reserves and find themselves unable to replace losses in the rifle companies. Operating with an extremely narrow margin, a rifle company's combat power declined precipitously without replacements. The loss of twenty men, not an unusual number in a day of combat, would reduce the firepower of a rifle company by 20 percent. Several days of heavy combat, after the field training battalions had been drained dry of men, would leave an infantry division with far less fighting power than would be expected from the gross numbers reported fit for duty. Maintaining a reserve in the field training battalion, supplied from the replacement battalions in Germany, was essential.

New men came from the Replacement Army in march battalions sent by train to their related divisions, filling up their field training battalions. The recuperating wounded were sent forward at more frequent intervals. Convalescent march companies ranged from 100 to 250 men, and men were often returned to duty in their former rifle companies.

About once a month, after the recruits then in the replacement battalions finished their advanced training, they were formed into a variety of units. Combat march battalions of 900 men with additional weapons and cadre were formed. The combat march battalions had the same tables of organization as infantry battalions and were considered fit to go into action. Standard march battalions had from 700 to 1,000 men, with smaller cadres and fewer weapons.

A combat march battalion and two march companies of returning wounded provided the divisional replacement battalion commander with approximately 1,200 trained men. However, in June 1944, when the Replacement Army deliberately delayed the forward movement of replacements despite Hitler's explicit order to get men forward in new and reconstituted divisions to oppose the second front as well as to hold off the Russians, the number of men in the Replacement Army increased. At the same time, the number of men in the field army dropped to only 4.7 million in June 1944. Far from straining every effort to provide replacements and create divisions to face the enemy, the Replacement Army was hoarding a large number of men in its training battalions.

In 1944 there were 371 infantry replacement battalions, eighty-four artillery replacement battalions, and sixty-two other combat replacement battalions for panzer, reconnaissance, antitank, and assault-gun units. These 517 battalions provided the Replacement Army commander with a force of more than one million well organized and equipped men. In June 1944 there were 1.7 million men listed as in training and 600,000 as convalescents, double the usual number, even though the preceding six months had been marked by a sharp reduction in casualties on the Eastern Front. The number of men held back from the front in the Replacement Army in June 1944 included at least 300,000 new men and 300,000 convalescents. The size of this force would not have been obvious, as the troops were spread across Germany in every city and town; the Replacement Army was therefore an ideal tool to seize control of Germany and keep the civilian population under control.

Depriving the divisions of these replacements resulted in a rapid decline in the fighting power of the German army, as there were no longer enough men to fire the machine guns when divisional replacement battalions were drained of manpower. Only about 2,100 men were assigned to the rifle companies in a division, where most of the casualties occurred. In active operations, rifle companies suffered heavily in a matter of weeks. Depriving a division of 1,200 replacements would reduce its frontline firepower by half. Field Marshal Erwin Rommel complained he had received only 10,000 replacements in the month following the Normandy invasion. Even in quiet sectors, each division normally would have received a thousand in that period, or at least 30,000 for an army group.

Once Hitler had regained control of the Replacement Army, many replacement battalions were sent directly to the front, either as part of existing reserve divisions under the command of the replacement division staffs reorganized as infantry divisions, or attached to existing infantry divisions. Other battalions were formed into "alarm" units, "block" units, and battle groups. The employment of replacement units in combat had been anticipated, and detailed plans existed for alerting replacement and training battalions in the event of an emergency. However, these plans were not implemented until August 1944.

The efficiency of the Replacement Army in providing units in an emergency is demonstrated by the reaction to "Market Garden," the September 1944 Allied operation intended to break through to Arnhem. Six replacement divisions from Military Districts V, VI, X, and XII were identified in the front line by the Allies. The process had begun with the assignment of the units ready for combat, under their replacement division and battalion numbers, with the suffix K. Men not ready for combat, recruits with fewer than four weeks' training, and convalescents unfit for duty remained under the command of units with their previous numbers. Later, the replacement divisions, regiments, and other units in combat received new numbers. The speed of the conversion was illustrated by the performance of the 180th and 190th Replacement Division staffs, which were alerted to the possibility of air landings at Arnhem on 15 September 1944. They were ready to march on 17 September and entered combat on 19 September. Half of the men in the replacement units controlled by these two divisions were unfit for immediate combat and were left behind. They were replaced by sweeping up all personnel in transit in the area, either going to or returning from leave or hospitals, or traveling for any other purpose.

Some replacement units formed special combat groups. In August the Infantry Officer Candidate School at Metz formed a combat group of three battalions and a howitzer company with 1,850 officer candidates; the new group took over a sector of the front opposing the U.S. 3rd Army. In September the officer candidates were commissioned and sent as replacements to other units. Their positions in the new combat group were taken by individuals swept up from every source; the group reached a strength of 4,000 men.

German infantry divisions were established in "waves" of varying numbers of divisions, each with the same table of organization and composition. Some divisions, however, were not part of waves. Other divisions were refitted at full strength according to organization tables, which took as much effort as building a new division. The creation of new divisions in the first four years of the war is summarized in Table 1.1.

It usually took two months to create a wave of divisions: assembling the cadres for the divisions, shipping in the recruits, training the new men, staging exercises, and sending the divisions to the field army. The final one or two digits of a division number often reflected the military district where the unit had been formed; for example, the 161st Division was formed in Military District I.

The First Wave comprised the twenty-six regular divisions formed in the 1930s. All of these divisions came from prewar German military districts, I through XIII, and the Austrian XVII Military District.

The Second Wave included sixteen infantry divisions formed in 1939 just before the outbreak of war (52nd, 56th, 57th, 58th, 61st, 62nd, 68th, 69th, 71st, 73rd, 75th, 76th, 78th, 79th, 86th, and 87th). All of these divisions were formed in thirteen German military districts— one each in ten districts and two each in three districts. Two of these divisions (58th and 79th) were initially equipped with French or other captured vehicles. The 52nd Division was formed in Kassel, in Military District IX, in the summer of 1939 from reservists who had served in the German army in the 1930s and had been discharged at the end of their terms. Elements of the division served in France and in Norway in the spring of 1940; in June 1941 they took part in the invasion of the Soviet Union.

The Third Wave, fifteen divisions of elderly reservists, was formed in August 1939 for occupation duty and was equipped with captured weapons and vehicles. Four military districts formed two divisions each, and seven others formed one each. The II, XIII, and XVII Districts did not form divisions. After the defeat of France, some divisions were furloughed from July 1940 to February 1941. In 1941 the units received German equipment and were placed in combat. The 206th Division was formed in Gumbinnen in Military District I and was assigned to the Eastern Front in June 1941 after the older men had been replaced by new recruits.

The fourteen divisions of the Fourth Wave (251st, 252nd, 253rd, 254th, 255th, 256th, 257th, 258th, 260th, 262nd, 263rd, 267th, 268th, and 269th) were formed in the summer of 1939 from recruits

Table 1.1
Forming New Divisions

Wave	Total	Type	Formed or Refitted	To Field Army
1	26	mobile	1933–1939	1939
2	16	mobile	August 1939	Sep 1939
3	15	occupation	August 1939	Sep 1939
4	14	occupation	Summer 1939	Sep 1939
5	5	occupation	Sep 1939	Nov 1939
6	4	occupation	Dec 1939	Jan 1940
7	14	mobile	Jan 1940	March 1940
8	14	mobile	April 1940	May 1940
9	9	home guard	April 1940	June 1940
10	9	incomplete		
11	10	mobile	Sep 1940	Nov 1940
12	6	light	Sep 1940	Nov 1940
13	9	occupation	Nov 1940	May 1940
14	8	occupation	Nov 1940	Jan 1941
15	15	occupation	April 1941	June 1941
	6	mountain	May 1941	June 1941
16		no data		
	9	security	July 1941	August 1941
17	4	mobile	Dec 1941	Feb 1942
	5	refitted	Nov 1941	Feb 1942
	10	motorized		
18	5	mobile	Jan 1942	April 1942
19	4	mobile	April 1942	June 1942
20	3	mobile	Aug 1942	April 1943
	17	refit and new	May 1942	Dec 1942
	23	refit and new	March 1943	Aug 1943
	18	refit and new	Dec 1942	June 1944
21	9	mobile	Nov 1943	Feb 1944
22	6	mobile	Jan 1944	June 1944
23	6	reserve	Jan 1944	June 1944
24	4	*Schatten*	Jan 1944	
25	6	mobile	Jan 1944	
26	4	*Schatten*	March 1944	
27	5	occupation	June 1944	
28	4	*Schatten*	July 1944	
29	17	infantry	July 1944	
30	6	infantry	July 1944	
31	5	*Schatten*	Aug 1944	
32	25	infantry	Aug 1944	

who had completed their training. Two districts, IV and VI, formed two divisions each. The remainder formed one, except for the I and XIII Districts, which did not form divisions in this wave. The divisions were equipped with German weapons and vehicles, except for two that were equipped with captured matériel. Most of these divisions manned the Siegfried Line, while the mass of the German army attacked Poland. The 251st Division was formed in Military District IX and entered combat in the Soviet Union in June 1941.

The five divisions of the Fifth Wave (93rd, 94th, 95th, 96th, and 98th) were formed in the fall of 1939 in Military Districts III, IV, IX, XI, and XIII. Their men were reservists, and they were equipped with captured weapons and vehicles. Most of the divisions, which held positions facing the Maginot Line in the winter of 1939 and in the spring of 1940, later served as occupation troops in France. In June 1941 they were transferred to the Eastern Front. The 93rd Division was formed in Military District III from reservists.

The four divisions of the Sixth Wave (81st, 82nd, 83rd, and 88th) were formed in autumn 1939 in Districts VIII, IX, X, and XIII with reservists. Equipped with Czech arms and vehicles, the divisions held quiet sectors in the French campaign; from June 1940 to January 1941 they were furloughed. In the spring of 1941 they were reassembled and sent to the East with modern weapons. In June 1941 the divisions received French vehicles and World War I German field artillery.

The Seventh Wave, of fourteen divisions (161st, 162nd, 163rd, 164th, 167th, 168th, 169th, 170th, 181st, 183rd, 196th, 197th, 198th, and 199th), was formed in January 1940 from Replacement Army units. Its divisions had German weapons but French or Czech vehicles. The 161st Division entered combat on the Eastern Front in June 1941.

The ten divisions of the Eighth Wave (290th, 291st, 292nd, 293rd, 294th, 295th, 296th, 297th, 298th, and 299th) came from ten districts in April 1940 with newly trained recruits of the class of 1918 (the male population cohort born in 1918). The divisions fought in France (only a month after being formed!) and in the Soviet Union in June 1941. The 295th Division fought in the Balkans in April 1941 and was sent to the Eastern Front in September 1941. An additional four occupation divisions were formed in this wave (554th, 555th, 556th, and 557th) but were later disbanded.

The Ninth Wave was formed in the spring of 1940 and consisted of nine divisions (351st through 359th); they were later disbanded. The Tenth Wave was started in the summer of 1940 with nine divisions numbered in the 307th to 341st range, but the divisions were never completed.

The ten divisions of the Eleventh Wave (121st, 122nd, 123rd, 125th, 126th, 129th, 131st, 132nd, 134th, and 137th) were formed in the autumn of 1940 from veterans and the class of 1920. The divisions were equipped with German weapons and captured vehicles. The 121st Division was formed in September 1940 in Military District I and first saw action in the Soviet Union in June 1941.

The six light divisions of the Twelfth Wave (102nd, 106th, 110th, 111th, 112th, and 113th) were formed in the autumn of 1940 with veterans and recruits from the class of 1920. The divisions had only two infantry regiments and were equipped with German weapons and French vehicles. The 102nd Division was formed in Military District II in October 1940 and entered combat in the USSR in August 1941.

The nine divisions of the Thirteenth Wave (302nd, 304th, 305th, 306th, 319th, 320th, 321st, 323rd, and 327th) were formed in November 1940 for occupation duties and lacked mobility. They were equipped with captured weapons and vehicles. The divisions had three infantry regiments but only three light field artillery battalions, with Czech guns. They had no reconnaissance battalions. The men were from twenty-four to thirty-five years of age. All except the 319th Division were assigned to the forces defending France in May 1941. During the summer of 1942, the divisions were equipped with German weapons for combat duty in the East. They began leaving France in June 1942, and by March 1943 they were playing a major role in Manstein's spring offensive.

The eight divisions of the Fourteenth Wave (332nd, 333rd, 335th, 336th, 337th, 339th, 340th, and 342nd), equipped with French weapons and vehicles, were formed beginning in November 1940 for occupation duty. The field artillery units had World War I German weapons. Later the units received German equipment and were used for combat in the East. All eight were assigned to France in June 1941. The 332nd Division was formed in Military District VIII in January 1941, went to France in August, and went to the Eastern Front in the spring of 1943.

The fifteen divisions of the Fifteenth Wave (702nd, 704th, 707th, 708th, 709th, 710th, 711th, 712th, 713th, 714th, 715th, 716th, 717th, 718th, and 719th) began forming in April 1941 for occupation duties. The divisions had only two infantry regiments, one field artillery battalion, and a reduced service component. There were only twelve machine guns in their rifle companies. Both arms and vehicles were French or other non-German types. The divisions of this wave were still on occupation duty in France in June 1944. The 702nd Division was formed in Military District II in April 1941 from older *Landesschutzen* men and was sent to Norway in May 1941.

Nine security divisions (207th, 213th, 221st, 281st, 285th, 286th, 403rd, 444th, and 454th) were created from infantry divisions in July 1941 with a single infantry regiment and older men armed with captured weapons. The divisions were to provide security for the rear areas in the Soviet Union. The 207th Security Division was formed from the 207th Infantry Division in the winter of 1940; it was sent to the Eastern Front in June 1941.

Six mountain divisions (1st through 6th) were formed before June 1941 with two mountain infantry regiments and were sent to the Eastern Front. Prior to June 1941 ten panzer divisions (11th to 20th) were formed by reducing the number of panzer regiments in each division from two to one while keeping the infantry component at two regiments. The 21st Panzer Division was formed from the 1st Cavalry Division. Ten motorized divisions were also formed (3rd, 10th, 14th, 16th, 18th, 20th, 25th, 29th, 36th, and 60th) from regular infantry divisions, reducing the number of infantry regiments to two and replacing horse-drawn transport with motor vehicles. The surplus infantry regiments were used to form the panzer divisions.

It is noteworthy that in the last four months of 1939, fifty-four divisions were formed in the Second through Sixth Waves, an average of nearly fourteen per month. A comparable program could have been carried out in 1944. In the months before the invasion of the Soviet Union an additional eighty-two divisions were formed. On the basis of this performance, the Replacement Army was fully capable of finding the resources for an additional sixty divisions between November 1943 and June 1944. The supply of weapons was no longer a serious hindrance; enormous stocks of captured Czech, Polish, French, and Russian weapons were available for security and occupation divisions. While motor vehicles were in short supply, there were ample numbers of carts and horses in France and Russia; horse-drawn transport was standard for infantry divisions anyway. Many of the divisions in Russia had adopted the local two-wheeled *panje* carts to navigate the poor dirt roads. Also, the Replacement Army had over three years' experience forming new divisions rapidly for anticipated operations, and the administrative structure was experienced in this process.

However, in February 1944 the creation of new divisions came to a halt. Only a few *Schatten* (shadow) divisions were formed between November 1943 and June 1944. The Replacement Army had a huge surplus of men, far more than would have been required for a prudent reserve, and more recruits and returning wounded were arriving in the replacement battalions every month. Given these facts, it must be concluded that the failure to create the sixty divisions needed to make the last desperate stand in the East and West was purposeful and not the result of circumstances.

2

The Strategic
Reserve in 1942

German military preponderance in Europe continued from September
1939 to December 1941. To maintain this hegemony, strategic
reserve divisions were created every spring for the summer campaigns.
The Germans created new divisions in the summer of 1939 to attack
Poland, in the spring of 1940 to attack France, in 1941 to attack Russia,
in 1942 to attack Stalingrad, and in 1943 to attack Kursk.

Creating groups of new divisions began in the summer of 1939.
After brief campaigns in Poland and France, Hitler relaxed his offensive stance. German divisions were scattered among the towns of
France, refitting and resting. Eighteen divisions were furloughed as
unnecessary for the conquest of Great Britain; the men were discharged and sent home. When the attempt to destroy the Royal Air
Force failed in autumn 1940, the planned invasion of Britain was called
off, and Hitler made known to army commanders his decision to attack Russia in the spring of 1941. In anticipation of an invasion of
the Soviet Union, on 13 July 1940 Hitler ordered the formation of
new divisions to expand the German army to 180. More than sixty
divisions were created in less than a year; most of them would see
combat in the first six months of the Russian campaign.

The expansion proceeded rapidly, and by December 1940 there were 188 divisions in the German army, including 140 in the field army (thirty-six in the East, eight in Norway, sixty-three in the West, and thirty-three in Germany). There were four SS divisions. The other forty-eight divisions were in the Replacement Army. In addition, twenty-six occupation divisions were formed, and eighteen divisions reduced to cadres after the French campaign were reconstituted within a few months in early 1941. These substandard occupation divisions, created using captured equipment, were to protect the shore against any immediate British threat while Hitler turned his attention to the East.

More mobile divisions were formed from January to June 1941. By 22 June 1941, there were 208 divisions in the German army: 120 on the Eastern Front, twenty-eight in reserve in the East, four in Finland, eight in Norway, thirty-eight in the West, seven in the Balkans, two in Africa, and only one left in Germany. The new divisions were formed in waves. Table 1.1 in chapter 1 lists the waves from the beginning of the war to August 1944.

The year 1942 began and ended with disaster for Germany. The Russians launched their winter offensive in December 1941 and inflicted the first major defeat on the German army in the Second World War. However, the German army showed remarkable resilience in coping with crises. In January 1942 the Germans, though hard pressed, were able to drive back the Red Army and stabilize the front. In the spring Army Group South decisively defeated the Soviet offensive at Izium and launched operation "Blau," which drove the Red Army back to the Volga. The German army reached the zenith of its power when the 6th Army reached the Volga at Stalingrad and the 4th Panzer Army occupied the oil fields in the Caucasus. To accomplish this resurgence the Germans had drawn on the strategic reserve of divisions in France and replaced them with new formations.

A close examination of the building of the strategic reserve in 1942 and its success reveals a picture in sharp contrast to later failures in the first half of 1944. After the defeat at Moscow in December 1941, work began immediately to create new divisions and refit weakened divisions for the campaign in the summer of 1942. Table 2.1 summarizes the divisions formed after January 1942 to July 1942.

The Seventeenth Wave (328th, 329th, 330th, and 331st Divisions) was formed in December 1941. They were called *Valkure* divisions and came from units of the Replacement Army, training personnel, recuperating wounded, and twenty-year-old recruits. The divisions were sent to Russia in February and March 1942. The 328th Division was

Table 2.1
Divisions Formed and Refitted, January 1942 to July 1942

Wave	Divisions	Type	Formed
17	4	mobile	December 1941
18	5	mobile	January 1942
19	4	mobile	March 1942
20	3	mobile	July 1942
	5	refit	November 1941
	17	refit & new	May 1942

organized at the Mielau training camp in Military District I, in East Prussia, in January 1942; its infantry regiments had been the 228th, 76th, and 207th Replacement Regiments. The 328th Artillery Regiment was formerly the 15th Artillery Replacement Regiment. In March 1942 the 328th Division was sent to Russia.

The Eighteenth Wave (383rd, 384th, 385th, 387th, and 389th divisions), the Rheingold divisions, were formed in January 1942 from the Replacement Army with new recruits, former students, and others previously exempted from military service, with an overall average age of twenty-seven years. The divisions were armed with German weapons and used civilian vehicles. The five divisions were sent to Russia in April 1942. The 383rd Division was organized at Camp Arys in France on 26 January 1942 from units in the Replacement Army and in April was sent to the 55th Corps of the 2nd Army at Voronezh, in the USSR.

The Nineteenth Wave (370th, 371st, 376th, and 377th divisions) was formed in the West in March 1942 as a group of mobile divisions by taking trained recruits and combat-fit men from occupation divisions in the West. The divisions were ready by June 1942 and were sent to the Russian front. The 370th Division was organized at Reims by the 1st German Army, taking recruits and training cadre from the 302nd, 304th, and 320th Divisions of the 15th Army. In June 1942 the 370th was sent to the 52nd Corps of the 17th Army on Mius River, in southern Russia.

The Twentieth Wave (38th, 39th, and 65th Divisions), known as *Valkure* II, was formed in July 1942 from companies in the replacement battalions. Its divisions, hastily assembled, were held in the West for months before being sent to the Russian front. The 38th Division was assembled from replacement companies from Military District II and III, at Munsterlager, in Germany, on 8 July 1942. It was sent to Holland later in the month and in August 1942 was assigned to the 88th Corps of Army Group D. In April 1943 the division was assigned to the 30th Corps of the 1st Panzer Army in southern Russia.

In addition to the infantry divisions formed in waves, the 22nd and 23rd Panzer Divisions were organized in France in September 1941, the 24th Panzer Division in December 1941.

The great summer offensive of 1942 on the Russian front was launched in the south. To provide a maximum number of troops there, divisions in the North and Center Army Groups were reduced to seven infantry battalions that were more manpower-effective in defense. Divisions in Army Group South were rebuilt to a full nine infantry battalions, as befitted their offensive mission.

Sixteen infantry divisions and one panzer division stationed in France in June 1941 departed for combat in the East between September 1941 and February 1942. Ten of these divisions were part of the Third Wave (205th, 208th, 211th, 212th, 215th, 216th, 223rd, 225th, 227th, and 246th), four divisions were from the Sixth Wave (81st, 82nd, 83rd, and 88th), and two from the Fourteenth Wave (339th and 342nd). In the summer of 1942 the 339th Division received German weapons, and in September it left for the East. The 342nd Division went to the Balkans in October 1941.

In the summer of 1942, fourteen divisions in France received German weapons and were sent to the East. The divisions, including eight divisions of the Thirteenth Wave (302nd, 304th, 305th, 306th, 320th, 321st, 323rd, and 327th Divisions) and six divisions of the Fourteenth Wave (332nd, 333rd, 335th, 336th, 337th, and 340th), had arrived in France in May and June 1941. The divisions had been formed in November 1940 for occupation duty, with three infantry regiments and three light artillery battalions equipped with Czech weapons. The men were from twenty-four to thirty-five years of age and armed with captured weapons and vehicles.

To provide temporary garrisons to replace divisions sent to Russia and to gain experience, four divisions of the Seventeenth Wave (328th, 329th, 330th, and 331st Divisions), the 383rd Division from the Eighteenth Wave, and four divisions from the Nineteenth Wave (370th, 371st, 376th, and 377th Divisions) were ordered to France in January and April 1942. All of these divisions were sent to Russia by June 1942, again to reinforce Army Group South.

France became a gigantic training ground for the creation or reconstruction of divisions that formed the strategic reserve of the German army and remained so until 1944. In addition to training new divisions in France, the German army conducted a rebuilding program, beginning in 1941. Divisions burned out on the Eastern Front and reformed in France from July 1941 to June 1942 are listed in Table 2.2.

Four infantry divisions (5th, 8th, 28th, and 71st Divisions) and the 2nd Panzer Division arrived in France in late 1941 and early 1942 for rebuilding or reorganization. These five divisions left France between February and July 1942 to take part in the Stalingrad campaign. An additional four infantry divisions (15th, 17th, 106th and 167th Divisions) and two panzer divisions (7th and 10th) were refitted in mid-1942 and returned to Russia in late 1942 and early 1943.

In addition to refitting divisions, the German army needed new divisions if it was to cope with the continued growth of the Red Army. The new German divisions were usually formed from single military districts. The recruits who were the bulk of the new divisions in 1942 were made available by drafting younger men to replace the losses suffered during the winter of 1941–1942. The class of 1922, boys who would reach twenty during 1942, were drafted between February and April 1942, about six months before normal induction. In March and April 1942, the class of 1923, the members of which would reach their nineteenth birthdays in 1942, were also drafted. Additional manpower

Table 2.2
Divisions Re-Formed in France, July 1941 to June 1942

Division	Refitted	Returned to Russia
2nd Panzer	September 1941	October 1941
5th	November 1941	February 1942
8th	January 1942	March 1942
28th	November 1941	March 1942
71st	November 1941	May 1942
15th	May 1942	March 1943
17th	June 1942	April 1943
106th	May 1942	March 1943
167th	May 1942	March 1943
7th Panzer	June 1942	January 1943
10th Panzer	April 1942	December 1942

came from 70,000 seventeen-year-olds who volunteered for the army. The youngest men went to reserve divisions; the others were sent either to Russia as replacements or to the new divisions.

The creation of the 65th Division is an example of how similar divisions could have been created in the spring of 1944, using the large number of men inducted as a result of Hitler's directive of 3 November 1943 to provide 1,000,000 men for the front (see Table 2.3).

The 65th Division was part of the Twentieth Wave, which also included the 38th and 39th Divisions. These divisions were formed from *Valkure* II companies and battalions created on paper in 1942 from the personnel engaged in training recruits. Upon the code word *Valkure,* the units were to assemble in prearranged larger units and move into action on short notice. A training battalion, for example, would list the names of men available to form a rifle company and gather them together for practice from time to time. Otherwise they continued their regular duties of training recruits. In July 1942 these "alarm" companies were called to form the three divisions of the Twentieth Wave.

Early in July 1942 a cadre of twenty-two officers, thirteen warrant officers, forty-two noncommissioned officers, and 193 men arrived in Camp Bitsch in Alsace-Lorraine to make quarters ready and to begin organizing the 65th Division. Between 7 and 15 July the mass of men

Table 2.3
Source of Manpower for the 65th Division (percent)

Bavaria	25
Rhineland	15
Palatinate	7
North Germany	3
Silesia	12
East Frontier	2
Baden and Wurtemburg	15
Mosel and Western	7
Styria	7
Central Germany	6
Sudeten Germany	2
Volksdeutsch (Polish)	1

arrived, and on 15 July 1942 the formal activation order was issued creating the division.

The men of the 65th Division came from all around southern Germany rather than from a single military district, as was customary. The new division consisted of the 145th and 146th Infantry Regiments, the 165th Tank Destroyer and Reconnaissance Battalion, the 165th Artillery Regiment, and service units. The II Battalion, 145th Infantry was formed by the 109th Replacement Battalion in Karlsruhe in Military District V; the III Battalion, 145th Infantry came from the 320th Replacement Battalion in Ingolstadt in Military District (WK) XII. The other troops came from various units in Military Districts VII, XII, and XIII.

Most of the equipment needed had been assembled by July 1942 in preparation for the division. Only three days after being formally activated, and though deficient in some respects, the 65th Division moved to Antwerp for training, the men by train and the vehicles by road. There were some technical problems. The motor vehicles were in poor condition, and there were no tools to repair them. The drivers needed more training. Half of the rifles and pistols were in poor condition, and there were no gunsmithing tools to fix them. The shortage statement for 27 July 1942 reported that there was no ordnance workshop. Also lacking were vehicles for the antitank company, antitank rockets, eighty-six motorcycles, three 37 mm guns, and twenty-two trailers. Despite these shortages, the division had an excellent supply of equipment for a new formation.

The 65th Division developed quickly as a result of the high quality of the officers and noncommissioned officers, who came from various units of the Replacement Army in Germany. Although half of the regimental and battalion commanders were not physically fit for combat, they were well able to provide combat training. Five of them had served in Poland and France, six in France and Russia, two in Russia; only three lacked combat experience. The younger officers had more recent battle experience. On 22 July, merely a week after activation, the division was missing only six junior-grade combat-unit officers, five medical officers, and seven veterinarians.

When the division was formed, about 25 percent of the privates were nineteen years old. The total number of enlisted men included 113 surplus privates, but the division was short 415 noncoms. Soldiers returning to duty who had been wounded in Russia made up about 33 percent of the men and provided a rich source of new noncoms.

The division was up to strength: the infantry battalions had 810 men each, the light artillery battalions 644, the antitank battalion 499, the engineers 339, and the signal battalion 431. The mixture of recruits and experienced combat soldiers resulted in rapid completion of training.

On 1 August 1942 the 65th Division detached 6,236 young soldiers whose training was complete and 657 returning wounded, a total of 6,993 of its 8,837 privates. The men were transferred to divisions being sent to Russia and were replaced by recruits. For the next nine months, the 65th Division served as a training division, receiving and training recruits and then transferring them to other divisions bound for Russia. In the week of 20 September 1942 the division received 3,255 recruits, of which 1,500 were nineteen years old or less. The arrival of 500 Poles who spoke little or no German made necessary the assignment of a Polish-speaking officer to each battalion to act as a morale and security officer.

The division transferred more men out than it received. On 9 October 1942 the 65th Division had 10,095 men, of which 7,855 were fit for combat. The division lacked fifty-eight officers, 407 noncoms, and 273 men. Many of the men had combat experience, as indicated by the award of Russian-campaign medals to 1,450 of them on 28 November 1942.

The steady turnover continued in November and December 1942, as a thousand fit men were exchanged for men with frostbite in the 39th Division. Many men suffered varying degrees of frostbite in the retreat in Russia during the winter of 1941–1942. Although painful when exposed to cold weather, frostbite did not prevent troops from serving in Western Europe, where temperatures seldom fell below freezing. While engaged in winter warfare training in 1947, I myself suffered a mild case of frostbite, but a friend in the same squad had been frostbitten before joining the army. Each night after exposure to cold he would groan in pain as his feet warmed up in his sleeping bag. When a German division in France was ordered to Russia, all its frostbitten men had to be transferred to other divisions.

Foreigners of German extraction were drafted into the German army but were classified according to their degree of loyalty to Hitler. The category *Volksdeutsch* III were men considered not reliable enough to use in Russia, and eighty of these men were transferred to the 65th Division from the 167th Infantry Division when it was ordered to the Russian front.

The example of the 65th Division is pertinent to the potential for creating new divisions in 1944. Shortages of equipment and supplies would not have occurred in 1944, as the rearmament program of Albert Speer, the armaments minister, had provided ample weapons for the army. Furthermore, there would have been an even greater supply of combat-experienced officers and noncoms among the recovering wounded. If the Germans were able to form divisions such as the 65th in a matter of weeks in 1942, they certainly could have in the critical period of 1944.

By September 1942 the struggle in southern Russia had bogged down. There apparently would be no rapid victory. Hitler ordered a series of programs to make men available for a new strategic reserve. On 12 September 1942 he ordered drastic measures to free men from service functions to replace the losses incurred in the summer campaign. More "hiwis," Russian volunteers, were assigned to the supply service to free Germans for combat duties.

To reduce the overall number of service troops, on 29 October 1942 a 10 percent cut was made in the total assigned to service units. Men were transferred from medical, transport, ordnance, postal, military police, and technical units. Some service units were reduced even more. The infantry division transport column was cut by a third, reducing the amount of munitions and supplies that could be carried; divisions became more dependent on daily supplies from army depots. The combat strength of infantry divisions was reduced, as the number of infantry battalions in each was cut from nine to seven. The normal fighting strength of the infantry company was reduced from 180 men to eighty.

In addition to the men made available by these reductions, wounded were returned to duty as soon as possible, and eighteen-year-old boys were used to fill divisions in France. The air force, the SS, and the navy were ordered to provide men for the army. Hermann Goering, commander of the Luftwaffe, protested a plan to use some of the nearly 2,000,000 air force men in the army; instead the air force created twenty field divisions that would fight as infantry in the army but remain under Goering's command. The new Luftwaffe field divisions were assembled from airfield defense regiments and antiaircraft battalions. All of their leaders, from generals to noncoms, came from the Luftwaffe, though they had little knowledge of land warfare; as a result, these divisions proved unsuccessful in battle. The Luftwaffe divisions were later incorporated into the army and were given experienced officers and noncoms, after which they performed well.

In September 1942, Hitler, still expecting to capture Stalingrad, the oil wells in the Caucasus, and Alexandria in Egypt, was planning the 1943 campaign. On 1 November he ordered the formation of forty-two fresh divisions to be ready by the spring of 1943. Twenty infantry divisions were to come from rebuilding battle-worn units from the Eastern Front. Seven panzer and motorized divisions were to be rebuilt in the West, while fifteen fresh infantry divisions were to be obtained from the armies in the West. With these additional divisions Hitler planned to demolish the Red Army in 1943.

The result of all of these programs was a startling increase in the army in the East. Hitler was informed of the Allies' decision at Casablanca to postpone the invasion of France until 1944. That knowledge freed him to strip the occupation force. During the summer of 1942, battered divisions from Russia were returned to France for rebuilding. In the second half of 1942, ten divisions were refitted, as listed in Table 2.4.

In December 1942 the German army in France had twenty-three mobile divisions, nine occupation divisions, and thirteen divisions. New divisions and the reserve (training) divisions were used for coastal defense in France, in addition to the occupation divisions. Divisions being rebuilt in France were the only reserve for the coastal defense.

Table 2.4
Divisions Refitted in France, July 1942 to February 1943

Division	Arrived	Departed
23rd	July 1942	February 1943
161st	November 1942	May 1943
257th	August 1942	April 1943
282nd	September 1942	May 1943
328th	January 1943	June 1943
1st Panzer	January 1943	June 1943
6th Panzer	July 1942	December 1942
1st SS Panzer	July 1942	February 1943
2nd SS Panzer	July 1942	February 1943
3rd SS Panzer	November 1942	March 1943

Soviet victories of early 1943 upset Hitler's plan; ten infantry divisions and five panzer divisions had to be sent to Russia by March 1943 to stop the Soviet offensive that had begun in November 1942. Of the seven rebuilt panzer divisions that were earmarked for the 1943 campaign, five went to Russia; the 26th Panzer did not complete its training, and the 10th Panzer was sent to Tunisia.

Eight divisions were created in the winter of 1942–1943 to replace the units transferred to Russia. Five new occupation divisions were formed and filled with limited-service men. Three new infantry divisions were formed with men from other divisions in the West; they in turn were replaced by new eighteen-year-old draftees.

A total of thirty-two divisions were lost between November 1942 and May 1943. Three panzer divisions, fourteen infantry divisions, and three motorized divisions were destroyed at Stalingrad. Two more panzer divisions, two infantry divisions, and two Luftwaffe field divisions were lost in the battles fought during the winter in the Ukraine. Tunisia cost three panzer divisions, a motorized division, and two infantry divisions. Of the thirty panzer divisions in the German army in November 1942, eight would be destroyed by May 1943—five in Russia and three in North Africa.

The events of 1942 had sorely tested the German army, but despite the combined efforts of the Soviet Union, Britain, and the United States, in January 1943 the overall German situation had not changed radically. North Africa was doomed, but the Italians and Germans would hold Tunisia for five more months. The Soviets had cut off the 6th Army at Stalingrad in November, but the Germans restored the situation in the Ukraine. In March 1943 German counterattacks inflicted repeated defeats on the Red Army as it attempted to exploit its earlier success.

The survival of the German army was made possible by the intervention of fresh divisions from France. The garrison in France was the primary source of the divisions that enabled the army groups in the Soviet Union to retake much of the territory lost in the winter offensive around Moscow in early 1942. Divisions from France reinforced Army Group South in April and May, giving it the resources to conquer the Ukraine and most of the Caucasus. Another group of divisions from France provided Manstein with the force to drive back the Red Army in the spring of 1943. Divisions from France enabled the Germans to hold Tunisia in the spring of 1943 as well as deal the Americans a costly defeat at Kasserine. In every instance, the key factor was complete, fresh divisions ready to enter combat to fill the vacuum left by divisions destroyed or weakened by enemy action.

The crucial factor was the ability of the German army to introduce new divisions after their opponents had committed most of their own resources. The reservoir of fresh divisions was refilled several times in 1942, giving the Germans the means to fight delaying actions that were costly to the Allies.

In contrast, no new divisions were created in the spring of 1944, even though there were 600,000 men available in replacement battalions in Germany—held there by the leaders of the Replacement Army. A strategic reserve was definitely needed in the spring of 1944 in expectation of the second front, as well as the anticipated Soviet summer offensive. The Replacement Army did not create a strategic reserve in the spring of 1944, because the German generals held back the troops as part of their coup to end the war. The lack of reserve divisions in 1944 led to the German disasters that followed in the East and the West.

3

Buildup for Kursk, February 1943 to June 1943

As previously noted, an annual event in the first four years of the war was the creation of a new strategic reserve every spring for the following summer campaign. In the spring of 1943 Hitler ordered the creation of a new divisions for the summer campaign, just as he had in the spring of the 1940 in preparation for the attack on France, in 1941 for the invasion of the Soviet Union, and in 1942 for the Stalingrad offensive.

The German army in the spring of 1943 was at one of its weakest levels of the war. Germany had suffered one defeat after another in Russia, North Africa, the Balkans, and in the air. Between November 1942 and March 1943 the German army in the East suffered nearly a million casualties but received only 500,000 replacements and returning wounded to replace losses. An additional 300,000 men from the Replacement Army were assigned to new units.

In addition to heavy German losses, the Russians had destroyed four satellite armies—the 2nd Hungarian Army, the 8th Italian Army, and the 3rd and 4th Rumanian Armies. Included in these armies were ten Italian divisions and brigades, ten Hungarian divisions, and eighteen Rumanian divisions. Of these thirty-eight units, only some Rumanian divisions remained in action with the Germans in the Kuban bridge-head by March 1943. Hitler lost confidence in the satellite troops and blamed them for the defeats of the winter; he ordered that Rumanians, Hungarians, and Italians be replaced with German troops. The loss in frontline strength was equivalent to at least 200,000 Germans.

In early 1943 the German high command estimated that 800,000 additional men would be needed to restore units to an acceptable strength. Hitler initiated a series of programs to replace the losses of men and equipment and restore the army for a major offense at Kursk.

The most obvious program was to accelerate the induction of young men into the army. Normally men were inducted in the year that they reached the age of eighteen. However, in 1943 the date of induction was pushed forward to provide replacements sooner. The class of 1924 (men born in 1924, reaching the age of eighteen in 1942) had re-ceived about six months' training and entered combat in the winter of 1942–1943. The class of 1925 (age eighteen in 1943) was drafted in May 1943 and sent to the front as early as September 1943 after only four months' training. The class of 1926 was drafted in the late fall of 1943 before reaching eighteen and was given only four months' training before being sent to units beginning in March 1944. The class of 1926 was available nine months earlier than would normally have been the case and made an enormous number of men available in the spring of 1944.

The changes in the induction and training schedule by June 1943 increased the Replacement Army to 1.5 million men in training and 300,000 convalescents, compared to 5,000,000 men in the field army and the SS. Heinrich Himmler increased the SS from 230,000 men in December 1942 to 433,000 in July 1943. The new SS divisions were formed with army cadre and, for the first time, conscripts instead of volunteers. Foreign volunteers were also accepted in increasing numbers.

Another program was designed to reduce the need for manpower. To make more men available for combat assignments, all infantry di-visions were, as noted previously, reduced to seven battalions. In 1942 Army Groups North and Center had reduced their divisions to pro-vide more men for Army Group South. With a few exceptions, that scaled-down organization was extended to all infantry divisions. In 1943 the 56th Infantry Division in Russia included the 171st, 192nd, and 234th Infantry Regiments, each of two battalions; the 56th Di-vision Battalion (two rifle companies, a cycle company, and a heavy weapons company); an antitank battalion (three motorized companies); and an Ost battalion (formed of Red Army prisoners). The service element included only one truck company. The 56th Division was reduced further after heavy losses in the summer of 1943. In October 1943 the division headquarters assumed command of Corps Detachment D, and the 171st and 234th Infantry Regiments were reduced to battalion-sized "regiment groups" in Division Group 56. In September 1944 the division was re-created from Corps Detachment D when the Replacement Army finally released its large reserves of men. The re-creation of the 56th Division could have been accomplished in the spring of 1944.

Panzer grenadier divisions were powerful units in 1943. They had two infantry regiments, each with three battalions of four companies. The division had no horses; everyone rode in or on a vehicle. This important factor meant that the entire division could move quickly by road for long distances, unlike the infantry divisions, which moved very slowly, either the infantry marching or the infantry moving by rail and the other elements by road, which led to endless confusion in crises.

The panzer grenadier division had a formidable arsenal of weapons. Each regiment had a cannon company, with six assault guns, and an antitank company, with nine guns. The division had a reconnaissance battalion, with seven armored cars, and four infantry companies in Volkswagens or on motorcycles. The antiaircraft battalion had eight 88 mm and eighteen 20 mm antiaircraft guns. The panzer battalion had 88 Panzer IV tanks. The artillery regiment had twelve 105 mm howitzers and eight 150 mm howitzers, four 88 mm guns, six rocket launchers, and twelve assault guns.

As an example, the 14th Panzer Grenadier Division in September 1943 included the 11th and 53rd Infantry Regiments, each with three battalions; the 14th Reconnaissance Battalion, the 14th Antitank Battalion, and the 14th Artillery Regiment (with three battalions). The service elements included two truck companies. However, the division had no tank battalion. Later the division was re-formed as a new-type infantry division with three infantry regiments of two battalions each, a fusilier battalion, and an artillery regiment of four artillery battalions.

Another type of division, also cut above the average, was the parachute division. The British at Cassino in Italy in 1943 and the Americans in Normandy in June 1944 found the parachute divisions to be stalwart opponents. Parachute divisions were similar to regular infantry divisions. Although few of the men actually had parachute training, they were trained as an elite group. The high level of morale of the young volunteers made the parachute divisions formidable foes in pitched battles of attrition. However, their lack of experience and transport reduced their value in more fluid situations.

The Luftwaffe field divisions, as noted above, were created to retain control of air force men being used as infantry. Although the men were young and fit, they lacked experienced leaders and training. These divisions were not comparable to parachute divisions and were little better than the occupation divisions until, as described, they were absorbed into the army and given veteran cadres of infantrymen to improve their competence.

Divisions also were created that made use of available manpower to perform special tasks. Occupation divisions were formed with men as old as forty-three to screen the French coastline against raids and to form an initial line of defense against a major invasion. However, once that invasion was launched and the crust was broken, they lacked the mobility to leave their fortress areas. Rather than retreating with the others in 1944, many of the occupation divisions remained bottled up in the Channel ports for the remainder of the war. The creation of these divisions began in September 1942; they had only two infantry regiments and reduced support and service units. They had far fewer motor vehicles and used a variety of captured weapons and equipment.

In September 1943, for example, the 716th Division, which was holding the Normandy coastline, had two fortress infantry regiments, the 726th and 736th. The designation "fortress" indicated that the men were physically below standard and not considered fit for mobile combat. Most of them were in their thirties and forties. The regiments did not have enough vehicles to move their weapons, which were permanently installed in fortifications. Each regiment had three infantry battalions but only a single antitank platoon of four guns. The divisional artillery regiment had only three batteries, with twelve obsolete French Model 1897 75 mm guns. Again, additional artillery was permanently emplaced in bunkers. There was only one self-propelled antitank company in the division. All of its service units were greatly reduced.

Despite their low combat worth in 1943, the occupation divisions could have been upgraded to infantry divisions by the addition of six combat replacement battalions, and the existing fortress battalions could have provided men to enlarge the service elements, supply officers and experienced noncoms for the new battalions, and replace men from the new battalions who could form antitank and infantry gun companies. By a process of exchanging men, a fusilier battalion (not part of a regiment) could have been formed from men drawn from the replacement battalions. The headquarters of two fortress battalions could have provided the nuclei for the headquarters of the fusilier battalion and the third infantry regiment. The remaining four fortress battalions could have been used to form a fortress brigade and continue screening the coast, as the division had done previously. Some upgrading of occupation divisions was done in early 1944 in the Balkans and in France.

The reserve divisions consisted of advanced training battalions transferred from Germany and assigned to occupation duties in France and Russia. Twelve such reserve divisions were sent to France in 1943 to replace infantry divisions sent to the East. Two reserve panzer divisions (155th and 179th), each reinforced with an artillery replacement battalion and an engineer company, were sent to France early in August 1943 as the mobile reserve. They were equipped with obsolete and captured tanks.

In July 1943 three reserve divisions were on coastal sectors, and more were proposed for this assignment. Reserve divisions were ordered to form regiment-sized combat groups for emergencies, but some divisions lacked the noncoms, vehicles, and trained soldiers to carry out this order. However, all of the reserve divisions formed several alarm battalions for defense against parachutists.

The conversion of the reserve divisions to regular infantry divisions would not have been difficult in 1944, and several were in fact converted. The reserve panzer divisions were used to re-create the panzer divisions lost at Stalingrad. The addition of several thousand "hiwis" would have provided the necessary service troops. By 1944 there was no shortage of weapons, and horse-drawn transport could have been requisitioned from the French.

Assignment to a reserve or field training division benefited the German recruit, who gained experience fighting the French underground or the Soviet partisans, a far more realistic form of training than any camp could provide. Fighting the partisans was practice, an intermediate stage of preparation for line combat.

A new draftee received his basic individual infantry training in a replacement and training battalion located in a barracks near his home in Germany. He was then sent either to a reserve division in the occupied territories or to a training unit behind the lines in the Soviet Union. When needed, he was assigned to a division field replacement battalion.

Another type of division was one that had suffered heavy casualties and was sent to France for refit. Often, in practice, only the rear elements and artillery moved to France; the remaining combat troops and any remaining equipment were transferred to other divisions. The rear element included one or two thousand specialists (signal men, medical, supply, ordnance, bakers, butchers, and veterinarians), artillerymen, and headquarters personnel. These troops formed the nucleus of a rebuilt division bearing the same number as the old division. Men returning from hospitals or furloughs and new inductees were sent to the unit, along with men from the navy and air force who had been retrained as infantrymen. This same process could have been used to transform the division groups in Russia into full-fledged infantry divisions.

Most of the men in the division had common ties and even family relationships, because as we have seen, the Germans related each division to a geographical area and to a specific replacement and training battalion. The result was an immediate development of unit spirit and combat efficiency. When the replacement battalions could not provide enough men, the shortfall was made up from other battalions in the same military district. A burned-out division having only a few thousand survivors could be re-formed within a few months.

Other divisions were created from the ground up using experienced cadre, returning wounded, transfers from other divisions, and new recruits from the Replacement Army. To re-form the divisions that had been destroyed at Stalingrad, existing divisions in France were required to provide cadres. The cadre men then had to be replaced as well. To replace cadre men sent to Stalingrad divisions from the 146th Grenadier Regiment of the 65th Division, the 146th Grenadier Regiment received an infantry company from the 265th Division.

The first step was bringing the men together, which, as we have seen with the 65th Infantry Division, took only a few weeks. Depending on availability, the divisions received weapons, vehicles, and other equipment in 1943. Often they trained with captured French and Soviet equipment, receiving new equipment just before being sent east. In 1944, as noted, there was no shortage of weapons.

All of these types of divisions were expedients to make the best possible use of German manpower as the nation faced new challenges in 1943. The plan for rebuilding the army was ordered on 4 February 1943 by Hitler. As a first priority, divisions in the East were to be provided with additional men and equipment in preparation for the summer offensive in 1943. The Russian offensives were halted by Manstein in March 1943, after which the spring thaw made further operations nearly impossible. The lull on the Eastern Front in the spring of 1943 was an important factor in the successful reconstruction of the German army. Many of the German panzer and panzer grenadier divisions were withdrawn from the front lines in April and provided with replacements and new armored vehicles.

The most immediate task in 1943, however, was to restore the balance in the Mediterranean theater after the loss of North Africa. In the spring of 1943 Hitler had sent units from France to Tunisia to fight a delaying action that tied down American and British divisions. Tunisia delayed the Western Allies for six months at a relatively small cost to the Germans. Six divisions (the 10th Panzer, 15th Panzer, 21st Panzer, 90th Motorized, 164th and 334th) eventually surrendered in Tunisia, plus elements of the 999th and Hermann Goering Divisions and the 1st Parachute Brigade.

All that was available to defend Sicily were remnants of these divisions and units in Naples and other ports that had been awaiting shipment at the time of the surrender. Replacements, returning wounded, base troops, and elements of the Hermann Goering Division not yet sent to Tunisia were used to re-form three divisions in June 1943. The Hermann Goering and the Sicily Division were formed in Sicily, and the Sardinia Division in Sardinia.

These three divisions were formed in a remarkably short time from a small nucleus. On 26 May 1943 the Sardinia Artillery Regiment had fewer than 140 men, formerly assigned to five artillery regiments captured in Tunisia. The 3rd Sicily Grenadier Regiment had gathered about 130 men from four infantry regiments and an artillery regiment. To rebuild these divisions was tantamount to creating entirely new units.

The Sardinia Division was organized for the defense of the island. On 7 July 1943 it was redesignated the 90th Panzer Grenadier Division. The Hermann Goering units in Sicily were reinforced to full division strength by July, re-forming the regiment that had been lost in Tunisia. The Reichsführer SS Brigade on Corsica was reinforced and became the 16th SS Panzer Grenadier Division in September 1943.

The Sicily Division was created in May in the same way, as it would have been possible to do in 1944 as well. Eight infantry replacement battalions, a battalion of artillery from the Hermann Goering Division, an army artillery battalion, and two newly formed artillery battalions were assembled to form the division. The Naples Antiaircraft Battalion and the 215th Tank Battalion (from army troops) were added later. On 1 July 1943 the few hundred survivors of the old 15th Panzer Division arrived, and the new unit was retitled the 15th Panzer Grenadier Division. Two months after being formed, the rebuilt divisions staunchly defended Sicily in July 1943. Because of the quality of the men available, the new divisions were ready to fight in two months or less.

In France, anticipating the movement of combat ready divisions to Russia, a program created eight occupation divisions, two infantry divisions, two parachute divisions, and two SS divisions. In addition the sixteen divisions lost at Stalingrad were re-created, for a total of thirty new divisions. Table 3.1 lists the divisions formed and refitted in France in 1943.

The 264th was a new static division. The 356th and 2nd Parachute were new divisions. The 13th SS was formed from Bosnian Moslem recruits. The 1st Parachute and 25th Panzer were refitting after Russian service. The 334th was being re-formed from remnants after the division surrendered in Tunisia. All of the rest were being re-formed from remnants left after the division surrendered at Stalingrad.

The sixteen divisions lost at Stalingrad were reestablished with their old divisional numbers. The tattered fragments of these divisions began to filter into France in March 1943. The men were survivors from the rear service elements, wounded who had been flown out, and men on furlough when the noose had closed around Stalingrad. The number of men left from the Stalingrad divisions was quite small—often the bakery company, the butcher company, and perhaps a medical company. Even returning wounded and those on leave seldom brought the total number up to a thousand.

The program began on 6 February 1943 with the order from High Command West (OKW) to re-form twenty divisions, including those lost at Stalingrad. On 11 February 1943 Hitler ordered that six of the divisions be completely rebuilt by 1 April, four more by 15 April, and the remainder by 1 September. Each division was to receive six new infantry battalions and nine artillery batteries.

The Replacement Army used demonstration troops from the military district training schools to form fourteen regiments, which were used to re-form seven of the divisions. On 15 February 1943 the military districts in Germany were ordered to comb through their

Table 3.1
New Divisions in France

Division	Arrived	Departed
44	March 1943	August 1943 to Italy
65	August 1942	August 1943 to Italy
76	April 1943	August 1943 to Italy
94	March 1943	September 1943 to Italy
113	April 1943	August 1943 to Russia
264	July 1943	November 1943 to Balkans
297	March 1943	September 1943 to Balkans
305	March 1943	August 1943 to Italy
334	July 1943	November 1943 to Italy
356	May 1943	November 1943 to Italy
371	March 1943	November 1943 to Italy
376	March 1943	November 1943 to Russia
384	March 1943	November 1943 to Russia
389	March 1943	October 1943 to Russia
3 Pz G	March 1943	July 1943 to Italy
29 Pz G	March 1943	July 1943 to Italy
60 Pz G	March 1943	January 1944 to Russia
1 Para	April 1943	August 1943 to Italy
2 Para	March 1943	August 1943 to Italy
14 Pz	March 1943	October 1943 to Russia
24 Pz	March 1943	August 1943 to Italy
25 Pz	September 1943	November 1943 to Russia
13 SS	August 1943	February 1944 to Balkans]

training schools to create a reinforced infantry regiment of three infantry battalions, an artillery battalion, an infantry gun company, an
antitank company, an engineer company, and a reconnaissance squadron. These 45,000 men were approximately half of the total school
troops in the Replacement Army. Organization began on 15 February,
and the regiments were ready to move only two weeks later, on 1
March. Fourteen districts produced fourteen regiments, which were
divided equally among the first seven Stalingrad divisions being re-
formed. District XVIII in Austria may have provided a regiment for
the 100th Jäger (light infantry) Division, being formed in the Balkans.

Six other Stalingrad divisions were rebuilt, at first only to regiment size, using returned wounded and eighteen-year-old recruits. Two motorized divisions were re-formed from the motorized training divisions, and a third was rebuilt using an infantry regiment withdrawn from another division. Two panzer divisions were generated from newly formed motorized infantry regiments, and a third was built slowly, using returned wounded and recruits.

During March and April 1943 about 150,000 replacements were sent to the Stalingrad divisions. By April 1943 seven infantry divisions had about 15,000 men each, and six more averaged 5,000 men each. The two motorized divisions had 15,000 men, while the third had only 5,000. The three panzer divisions had 10,000 men each but a total of only seventy-eight French Somua and Hotchkiss tanks, revealing the shortage of weapons at this point.

On 13 March OKW complained that the rebuilding of the Stalingrad divisions was being slowed because the East was given preference for rifles, machine guns, antitank guns, and artillery. The 14th, 16th, and 24th Panzer, and the 60th Motorized had received no German weapons, while the 3rd Motorized and 29th Motorized were missing 25 percent or more of their weapons.

On 23 March 1943 Army High Command (OKH) informed OKW that by the middle of April all Stalingrad units would have received a quarter of their German weapons and that the remainder would follow. In the interim, 25,000 French rifles and 4,000 French light machine guns were offered for use in training.

Large numbers of replacements flowed to the new divisions. The 44th Division received 10,000 men by 5 April; the 76th about 3,500 between 6 and 12 April; the 113th about 3,000 in the first week of April; the 305th about 10,000 on 5 April; and the 24th Panzer about 7,500 on 13 April. However, recruits were not available to fill the 384th Division.

By mid-April some of the Stalingrad divisions had full complements of men. Those with the most men had benefited from the inclusion of the fourteen regiments formed from school troops. Training battalions had also been used to re-create the new divisions. By 1 July 1943 most of the twenty Stalingrad divisions had been filled with men, but they lacked full inventories of vehicles, weapons, equipment, and even horses. In August many of these divisions were sent to Italy. Hitler relied almost entirely on the rebuilt units and new parachute divisions to defend Italy. The panzer and panzer grenadier units were ready by September 1943.

Five of eight new occupation divisions (343rd, 344th, 346th, 347th, 348th, 16th Air Force, 17th Air Force, and 18th Air Force) were created from cadres provided by the units leaving for the Soviet Union. The divisions ordered to Russia sloughed off their older men to create fortress infantry regiments that made up the five army occupation divisions. (This procedure is basically that proposed below for the spring of 1944, but forming fortress brigades rather than occupation divisions.) In 1943 the 346th Occupation Division was formed from cadres from the 257th, 319th, 320th, 304th, and 332nd Divisions, with fillers from Military District VI and IX. The new division had five fortress infantry battalions and two artillery battalions, plus engineers, and signals and service assets. The total strength of the 346th Division was about 7,000 men. The three new air force occupation divisions were formed in Germany from airfield protection regiments and anti-aircraft gunners who had been replaced by children and Soviet prisoners of war. The divisions had minimum service elements.

The two new infantry divisions (326th and 338th) were formed from *Kriemhilde* alarm units from the Replacement Army. These units were originally to be formed for use in emergencies. In May 1943 the two divisions exchanged their younger men for elders and were reclassified as occupation divisions. Their regiments received the fortress designation.

The two new parachute divisions were produced by splitting the 7th Flieger Division, which had been burned out on the Eastern Front, and adding various air force elements as well as new recruits. The two new SS divisions were made up of young graduates from the Hitler Youth, many seventeen years old. Leaders from the Hitler Youth served as cadre. More time was needed to work these divisions into fighting units, because the men were young and lacked a good cadre.

To defend France against a possible invasion, the OKW on 5 February 1943 set out to establish a reserve of six to eight mobile divisions. The core of the reserve consisted of the 1st Panzer, 26th Panzer, and the 326th, 338th, 342rd, 344th, 346th, 347th, and 348th Infantry Divisions. The infantry units were all new occupation divisions formed in October 1942 with limited mobility and older men. Priority was given to the 9th and 10th SS Panzer Divisions and the 24th Panzer Division, which were to be ready for combat by 1 June. The target for 1 April was four additional fully equipped and combat-ready mobile divisions.

By April 1943 there were nineteen occupation divisions, the Stalingrad divisions, some forming divisions with a minimum of training, and ten training divisions in France. High Command West was ordered to prepare six divisions for combat service in Russia by 1 May. On 17 February 1943 the 76th, 94th, and 305th Stalingrad Divisions in France were alerted to provide battle groups to assume the duties of seven divisions that were to be sent to the USSR—the 17th, 38th, 39th, 106th, 161st, 182nd, and 257th Divisions. The 44th and 113th Divisions were also required to take on assignments when the departing divisions left in late March. The rebuilding program in France in the spring of 1943 provided divisions for both the defense of Italy and the reinforcement of the armies preparing for the attack on Kursk.

Hitler's plan of 4 February 1943 was mostly carried out. Between June 1942 and August 1943, the Germans created forty-seven new divisions in the West and rebuilt eight that had suffered heavy losses on the Eastern Front. Beginning in November 1942, twenty-six divisions were sent to the East; one was sent to Denmark for further training; two went to the Balkans; and fifteen were sent to Africa and Italy. The German army in Russia had a net gain in manpower between April and June 1943 of 215,000 men, compared to a net loss of 319,000 from January to March 1943.

This ambitious program required nearly a million new men for the army. About 300,000 replacements came from the class of 1925, which was conscripted in early 1943. On 22 January 1943 Hitler ordered the conscription of 200,000 men previously exempted for essential civilian occupations, business, and mining. On 8 January 1943 he ordered the drafting of 100,000 men aged thirty-eight through forty-two and 100,000 in the twenty-one through thirty-seven age group. There not being enough physically fit men in the older age groups, an additional call was made on 10 March 1943 for 112,000 men in the forty-three through forty-six age groups.

On 12 May 1943 the OKH ordered a sorting out of age groups in the infantry divisions. Combat troops in regular infantry divisions were to be from eighteen to thirty-six years old. Troops in service units must be thirty-seven years or older. Younger men combed out of service units were transferred to combat units and replaced by older men. Men recuperating from wounds were assigned to divisions in France to replace men sent to Russia. As many as 45,000 recuperating wounded per month were assigned to divisions in the West rather than remaining in replacement battalions in Germany until they were fully recovered.

Many programs were carried out to provide more men for the combat units—combing fit men from service units, reducing the size of divisions, using air force men as infantry, eliminating occupational deferments, and assigning hiwis to service units. Russians were employed as soldiers in Italy and the Balkans, and replaced able-bodied men in antiaircraft units in Germany. German grooms for horses, supply clerks, and teamsters were retrained as infantrymen and replaced by Russian hiwis. Recruits completing their basic training in Germany were sent to reserve divisions for occupation duty.

Young people were required to serve two years, rather than one, in the German Labor Service. Some were assigned to man antiaircraft guns, freeing 500,000 men from antiaircraft defense units for transfer to the army or to air force field divisions. Some German Labor Service youths formed battalions of light guns, as well as helping in the heavy batteries. Beginning on 20 September 1942, boys and girls of aged fifteen and sixteen were enrolled as flak helpers. On 25 January 1943 Hitler ordered boys of fifteen to be excused from school to serve in the antiaircraft units. In February 1943, 100,000 Russian prisoners were ordered into the antiaircraft service. The children did the sighting and technical work, while the Russians handled the ammunition, supervised by a small number of older soldiers. Attempts to recruit French, Dutch, Belgians, and Danes to man antiaircraft guns in their countries were not successful.

More foreign nationals of German descent previously exempted from service because of suspected antagonism to Germany were reclassified from Category *Volksdeutsch* IV (hostile to integration into the German state) to the less suspicious *Volksdeutsch* III (racial Germans deemed amenable to German culture). The newly reclassified men were then drafted. Many spoke no German and were noticeably unreliable and quick to surrender.

The OKH prohibited the assignment of Polish *Volksdeutsch* III to units on the Eastern Front on 31 March 1943, but many were sent to Tunisia after only three weeks' basic training. Many probably had prior training in the Polish army, as the Germans were calling up men from the classes of 1900 through 1925 (eighteen through forty-three years old). Because the Poles spoke no German, they were trained together but were scattered when assigned to combat units. The Germans limited to two the number assigned to any given infantry section.

The Germans also called up *Volksdeutsch* in Yugoslavia from the classes of 1919, 1920, and 1921 (twenty-two through twenty-four-year-olds). Because most of them spoke very little German, they had to be trained together. After training the Slavs were assigned to combat units. The II Battalion, 756th Mountain Regiment in Tunisia, had forty Yugoslavs and ten Rumanians.

The prisoner of war camps were a large potential source of manpower. The September 1943 table of organization for the infantry division increased the number of hiwis to 2,005, about one-seventh of the total men in the division. An example of the impact of the use of Russians was the experience of the 134th German Infantry Division. In January 1943, fit Germans were combed from the artillery regiment and supply units and replaced with hiwis. A special school was established to retrain the Germans as infantrymen. By March 1943 additional hiwis joined the 134th Ost Battalion, and two platoons of hiwis were attached to the 134th Pioneer Battalion. By April 1943 2,300 hiwis had been assigned to the 134th Division, and a further 5,600 prisoners of war had been attached for labor details.

The hiwis were used most often to drive and care for the ever-present horses in German units. The basic unit for providing supplies to the infantry was the horse-drawn vehicle squadron, which could transport sixty tons in *panje* wagons, small Russian carts. On 25 August 1943 the table of organization of these units included two officers, twenty-seven German noncoms, seventy-one German privates, and 159 hiwis. The unit had 381 horses and 176 wagons. All of the hiwis were armed with rifles for security.

At the beginning of 1943, 176 battalions of Soviet prisoners had been formed to provide occupation troops in the West, Italy, the Balkans, and Russia. More than 52,000 Russians were recruited into larger combat units, including the Pannwitz Cossack Corps, of two divisions. During the summer of 1943, two new divisions were formed: the 162nd Infantry Division, with German cadre, which was sent into combat against the British in Italy; and the 1st Cossack Division, which fought against the partisans in Yugoslavia. The Russian Liberation Army created in June 1943 eventually included two additional divisions.

Children, Poles, and Soviet prisoners were all used to reinforce the army. The impact of the massive German rebuilding program can be appreciated by examining the results in a few sample divisions. The Gross Deutschland Division was rebuilt in early 1943 for the battle at Kursk. One of the rifle groups of the Fifth Company included an experienced noncommissioned officer, two corporals in their twenties, a machine gunner just past eighteen, and his assistant, not quite seventeen. The three riflemen were an older Czech, a Sudeten, and an

Alsatian, the latter two nineteen. The second machine-gun team consisted of a veteran and a terrified boy. The group had two MG42s; two men were armed with machine pistols, and the remainder had rifles. The group had four veterans, three young recruits, and three non-Germans, two of whom were nineteen.

The 260th Division, assigned to a quiet sector on the Russian front in 1943, is an example of an average division. In 1942 it received 9,800 replacements, more than its total of 5,645 losses (715 killed, 99 missing, and the remainder wounded). In February 1943 the two regiments had almost 2,500 men each, compared to the allotted strength of 3,000 men. The division had an Ost battalion and a tank company equipped with captured Russian tanks and armored cars.

Although the 134th Division was short of leaders in early 1943, lacking more than 10 percent of its officers and about 5 percent of its noncoms, it was well equipped, with 80 percent of its authorized vehicles and weapons. It had 515 trucks, compared with the authorized 537; thirty-one antitank guns (most of them 37 mm), compared with the twenty-two 75 mm antitank guns authorized; thirty-six howitzers, compared with forty-eight; and 448 light machine guns, compared with 614. The 134th Infantry Division on 22 April 1943 had 14,100 combat-fit Germans, 1,100 limited-service men, 2,300 Russians in its service elements, and 5,600 Russian prisoners working as laborers attached to the division.

By July 1943 the German army had been greatly strengthened in spite of the loss of thirty-two divisions at Stalingrad, in the Ukraine, and in Tunisia. In addition to replacing losses, a large number of divisions were formed or rebuilt in 1943 (see Table 3.2).

The 38th, 39th, 282nd, and the 26th Panzer were new divisions. All of the other divisions were units refitting after fighting on the Eastern Front.

The success of the rebuilding effort can be judged by a review of the resources available for the Kursk offensive in July 1943. Most of the German army was on the Russian front. On 1 July 1943, of the 3,142 tanks available to the Germans, 2,269 were in the East, along with 997 of the 1,422 assault guns and 500 of the 600 tanks considered obsolete. Of the total of 276 divisions in the German army, 186 were on the Russian front, along with seven of the twelve SS divisions. Between 1 April and 30 June 1943, nearly 350,000 men were added to the army to replace only 134,000 losses. By 1 July 1943 the total number of men in the army had increased to 4,484,000, from fewer than 4,000,000 a year before.

Table 3.2
Divisions Formed and Rebuilt in France in the First Half of 1943

Division	Arrived	Departed
15	May 1942	March 1943
17th	June 1942	April 1943
23rd	July 1942	February 1943
38th	August 1942	April 1943
39th	August1942	April 1943
106th	May 1942	March 1943
161st	November 1942	May 1943
167th	May 1942	March 1943
257th	August 1942	April 1943
282nd	September 1942	May 1943
328th	January 1943	June 1943
1st Panzer	January 1943	June 1943
6th Panzer	July 1942	December 1942
7th Panzer	June 1942	January 1943
10th Panzer	April 1942	December 1942
16th Panzer	March 1943	June 1943
26th Panzer	October 1942	August 1943
1st SS Panzer	July 1942	February 1943
2nd SS Panzer	July 1942	February 1943
3rd SS Panzer	November 1942	March 1943

All of the best divisions were centered on Kursk, about fifty, including sixteen panzer or panzer grenadier. All of the new Panther tanks and the Tigers were sent to Kursk. By 5 July 1943 the Germans had concentrated for a single campaign their most awesome armored force of the war.

Many of the divisions had been transferred from France or from the Rshev salient in early 1943. All of the divisions had been reinforced during the preceding three months. Of the total of fifty German divisions that would take part in the Battle of Kursk, nine came from the Rshev salient; thirteen had been transferred from France in the previous six months; and ten were panzer divisions that had been transferred from the reserves of Army Groups South and Center. Only seven were combat-weary units that held the quiet 2nd Army sector.

At Kursk the Germans tried to regain the initiative, to make use of their superior fighting ability in fluid situations. They could not afford to sit and wait for the Russians; instead, they selected a battlefield and launched a massive attack. Germany's greatest hope was to keep the Soviets off balance, as Manstein had done in the spring of 1943. Hitler continually referred to the need to retain the initiative as the reason for launching the offensive at Kursk.

Despite the outstanding achievement in rebuilding the panzer troops, the Germans failed to provide sufficient infantry to support the Kursk offensive. The diversion of the Stalingrad divisions to Italy contributed to the shortage of infantry. As the battle unfolded, the critical lack of infantry divisions played an ever-increasing role in the failure of the campaign. Repeatedly panzer divisions were tied down protecting the flanks of attacking forces, the proper role of infantry divisions. The 4th Panzer Army was chronically short of infantry to secure its flanks, and panzer divisions were diverted from the spearheads to hold both the eastern and western flanks. When Manstein asked the 2nd Army commander for infantry divisions, the commander pleaded that his weak divisions were already stretched too thin and sent none. The eastward drive of the 3rd Panzer Corps, which could have created a crisis for the 7th Soviet Guards Army, was aborted because of lack of infantry. A panzer corps of Army Detachment Kempf was forced to turn north to plug up the gap that had developed between it and the 4th Panzer Army, a gap that would never have developed had there been enough infantry.

After the failure to cut off the Soviet forces at Kursk by double pincer attacks, Hitler wisely called off the attack and prepared to stem the tide of Soviet offensives that would ultimately drive the army back to the Dnieper River.

The shortage of infantry divisions at Kursk was due largely to the Allied threat in the Mediterranean. The Stalingrad divisions were diverted to defend Italy, as noted, rather than returning to the East. Recreating these divisions had absorbed a major portion of the available replacements. Without these replacements the infantry divisions on the Russian front could not be upgraded from seven to nine battalion divisions. Some of the German divisions in Russia were even smaller. Thirteen of the infantry divisions at Kursk had only six rifle battalions, and one had only three battalions. Without the missing divisions and battalions, there was not enough infantry to support the panzer advances.

The Germans completed a remarkable rebuilding program in the first half of 1943. Twenty-six of the thirty-three divisions lost at Stalingrad and in Tunisia were re-formed; ten new occupation divisions were formed (five in France and five in Norway); four occupation divisions in the Balkans were upgraded to combat divisions by replacing older men with more fit younger men; four new SS divisions were formed; the air force formed fourteen additional field divisions; the 7th Flieger Division was re-formed as two new parachute divisions; and most of the panzer divisions on the Eastern Front were rehabilitated behind the front prior to July 1943. A total of sixty new and upgraded divisions were created in 1943, and more than twenty panzer divisions were refitted.

In reviewing the reconstruction programs of 1943, we can see clearly the techniques by which a stronger rebuilding program could have been instituted in early 1944. More men were available in 1944, and weapons were plentiful. The same organizations that were used to create new divisions in 1943 were available in the spring of 1944— occupation divisions that could have been upgraded with the infusion of younger men; burned-out divisions that could have been reconstituted with a half-dozen replacement battalions; reserve divisions that could have retained their trainees and formed the missing service and weapons units; and new divisions that could have been built with cadres from existing divisions. If sixty divisions could be created in 1943 with a fewer men and fewer weapons, why was a similar program not possible in the spring of 1944?

4

The Ukraine and Italy, June 1943 to February 1944

The invasion of Sicily and the Soviet offensive following the failure at Kursk created emergencies in both East and West. In the summer of 1943 a fresh group of divisions from France had given the Germans the means to launch the Kursk offensive, but the Germans failed to break through and were forced to withdraw in a few weeks, and in Sicily the only possible strategy was a delaying action. In the Ukraine the Red Army was finally held at the Dnieper River line, when another group of German fresh divisions arrived to restore the balance.

The impending invasion of Italy diverted most of the strategic reserve in France to contain the Western Allies, while Soviet attacks in the Ukraine absorbed the few divisions left. In past summers German attacks had created crises within the Soviet Union; for months all of the energy of the Red Army would be needed to contain the offensive. The winter offensives of the Red Army had been brought to a halt by the spring thaws.

In 1943, however, the Soviets contained the German attack at Kursk in a matter of weeks and launched a series of operations that drove the Germans back to the Dnieper River. In late July probing attacks by the Soviets in the south at the Mius River front absorbed all of the local German reserves. Then, on 3 August 1943, the Russians launched a major offensive in the center, driving seventy miles in five days, followed by another attack in the south on 13 August 1943. The Russians advanced steadily during August and September and crossed the Dnieper River by the end of September.

An example of the weakening of the Germans in the East is the decline of the 3rd Panzer Army. A division at full strength could hold a front about ten miles wide, but by mid-July 1943 the weakened divisions of the 3rd Panzer Army were holding as much as seventeen miles each, with only about 3,000 combat soldiers per division, or one soldier for eighty yards. In May 1943 the Third Panzer Army had 292,000 men, but by September it had been reduced to 230,000, and in October to only 200,000. Four poor Luftwaffe field divisions held over fifty miles. When the Russians attacked on 6 October 1943, the 2nd Luftwaffe Division broke and ran, leaving a hole ten miles wide on the German front. The entire army had to pull back. By November a great deal of territory had been lost.

Hitler needed a second group of fresh divisions in August, and he needed them at once. In July 1943 many of the divisions rebuilt in the spring in France had fought at Kursk, and in August the Stalingrad divisions were sent to Italy. After July 1943 the demand for replacements grew more intense, both to replace losses and to form new divisions. Three operations—the Battle of Kursk, the invasion of Sicily, and the Russian late-summer offensive—cost men who now had to be replaced.

The armies in the East received men not only from the Replacement Army but also from divisions in France. During the late summer of 1943, the Germans sent each month 20,000 combat-ready replacements from the divisions in the West to fill the divisions in the East; between September and November, 90,000 men were sent from west to east. However, by 1 September 1943 the total strength of the western army had decreased to 770,000, including the SS, Luftwaffe divisions, service units, and security troops.

During 1943 the Replacement Army maintained a healthy average of about a million men: training personnel, recruits in training, men recuperating from wounds, and trained men awaiting movement to the front. During the year ending October 1943, it sent an average of 100,000 replacements per month to the Eastern Front. Smaller numbers were sent to the Mediterranean and to the West. With a maximum of six months' training or recuperation for the average soldier, the Replacement Army could produce 1.5 million trained men yearly. At the rate of 10,000 men per year per division, 1,500,000 replacements could maintain 150 divisions in active combat. Divisions not actively engaged needed few replacements.

To replace losses and form new divisions, the army requested the induction of 700,000 additional men for the second half of 1943. A total of 1.5 million men were drafted in 1943 and processed through the replacement system. To provide for an increased supply of replacements, the Germans drafted young men of the class of 1926 (seventeen years old) in the fall of 1943. Older men, between fifty and sixty, were drafted to provide replacements for younger men in noncombat jobs. Those with hearing and stomach ailments were drafted and formed into "ear" and "stomach" battalions, for occupation duty. To replace the workers conscripted from industry, 200,000 Russians were sent to the coal mines and 500,000 Italians to other industries, permitting the release of 850,000 Germans previously exempted from service. In September 1943, in desperation, the exemption of the last or only son of a family was canceled, along with the exemption of fathers of five or more children. The railroad and the border service were combed for additional men.

Rebuilding the panzer divisions in the East in June 1943 and the Stalingrad divisions in the West in the summer of 1943 had strained German production. The total output of tanks, assault guns, and self-propelled antitank guns for January through April 1943 averaged only 600 per month. The position with regard to other weapons was equally critical. The Stalingrad divisions were training with substandard equipment—French rifles and machine guns, French 75 mm guns remaining from World War I, and Russian 122 mm howitzers captured in 1941. This situation would change in 1944.

With the objective of freeing 500,000 men from industry for the army, on 26 July 1943 Hitler consented to place under Speer all production, military and civilian. The induction of an additional 800,000 men into the army created a shortage of manpower in industry in early 1943. As noted, the men inducted into the army were replaced in part by conscripted labor from the occupied countries, but the results of previous attempts to use forced labor had not been altogether successful. Beginning in the spring of 1943 Speer shrewdly offered certain French factories the opportunity to produce civilian goods for Germany in exchange for protection of their employees from forced labor in Germany. In this way Speer believed he could make better use of French manpower. In July 1943 the first protective contracts were signed with a number of French firms. Factories in Belgium, Holland, and other countries followed, agreeing to produce civilian goods for Germany. With nonmilitary goods arriving from outside, German factories were converted to producing military supplies.

Hitler was concerned that the civilian economy not be disrupted, lest the German people lose faith in him. With Speer's plan, the mobilization of 1943 did not have a severe impact on the German domestic economy. In October 1943 Speer ordered the transfer of 1.5 million of the 6,000,000 German workers from civilian to military work. By December 1943, three months later, Speer's reorganization of German industry was successfully accomplished. By December a million men were added to the army, and unprecedented numbers of weapons were being produced.

The additional manpower available to the army was not all of high quality. To make better use of limited-service men, the Germans created more occupation divisions to replace infantry divisions in France, Norway, and other theaters. In May 1943 there were five occupation divisions. An order of 12 May 1943 outlined a massive buildup program. Eight occupation divisions were to be formed in France and two more in Norway. Two infantry divisions were to be reorganized as occupation divisions by exchanging younger soldiers for older men, to bring the average age near thirty-six years.

The new occupation divisions consisted of seven battalions in three regiments, with smaller service elements. The eight divisions were built on cadres from divisions burned out in Russia. The remnants of the 323d, 340th, and 377th Divisions provided approximately 5,000 men each, and 2,000 men each came from the 298th, 385th, and 387th Divisions. These cadres arrived beginning on 15 July 1943, after the men had returned from furloughs after service against the Russians. Three divisions were formed two weeks after the arrival of the cadres on 1 August, four more on 15 August, and the final division on 1 October. The two Norwegian divisions were formed from divisions and units in Norway. The conversion of the 326th and 338th Divisions from infantry to occupation status was completed by 1 August 1943. The nineteen occupation divisions were available by September 1943. Because they were of little use other than in coastal defense, only four additional such divisions were formed during the rest of the war. The rapid formation of twelve occupation divisions indicated again the ability of the Replacement Army to create divisions.

The reserve divisions training men in France were also used to bolster the defense and release infantry divisions for use elsewhere. Some of the reserve divisions were manning the coastal sectors along with the occupation divisions. On 10 September the 182d and 189th Reserve Infantry Divisions were transferred from the Replacement Army and placed directly under the command of Field Marshal Gerd von Rundstedt.

The standard German infantry division in 1943 was a self-contained formation made up of infantry and appropriate supporting arms; it had 10,000 men or more, including 2,000 hiwis in the service element. To save additional manpower the infantry divisions were streamlined in late 1943, giving them more firepower while reducing the number of men. More weapons were given to fewer men. The infantry regiment was reduced from three to two battalions. The divisional reconnaissance battalion was replaced by a standard infantry battalion, called a fusilier battalion. On 4 October 1943 the streamlined divisions were designated as infantry divisions (new type).

The new organization was more efficient. The former organization of three regiments with three battalions usually resulted in two regiments in front, each with two battalions in the first line and a third in the second; the third regiment was held in reserve in a third line. The result was four battalions at the front and five in reserve. To do otherwise would disrupt the chain of command. With seven battalions, two regiments placed four battalions in the first line as before. The third regiment with two battalions was in the second line, and the fusilier battalion could either form the third line or reinforce the other two lines. The result was the same four battalions at the front, but the needlessly strong reserve was reduced from five battalions to three. An added benefit was that the regimental cannon and antitank companies supported two battalions rather than three.

At the same time the number of men in the infantry battalion was reduced from the previous 820 men, with fourteen men in each rifle section, to 708 men, with only nine men in the section. The allotment of machine guns and other heavy weapons, on the other hand, was increased. The new battalion had fifty-one light machine guns, twelve heavy machine guns, six medium mortars, and four heavy mortars. The basic unit was the rifle group of nine men with one or two MG42 light machine guns. On 9 September 1943 two 80 mm mortars replaced the 50 mm mortar in the rifle company, and the battalion machine-gun company was equipped with six 80 mm mortars and four 120 mm mortars.

Each of the three regiments had an antitank company, with twelve towed 50 mm antitank guns, and a cannon company with eight "infantry guns," short-barreled howitzers. The division had an antitank battalion with twelve 88 mm or 75 mm guns, eight to fourteen self-propelled 75 mm antitank guns, and some 20 mm self-propelled anti-aircraft guns. The divisional artillery regiment had thirty-six 105 mm howitzers and twelve 150 mm howitzers.

Most of the transportation was horse drawn. Only the antitank guns and some of the service elements were motorized. The only motor vehicles in the infantry battalion were five half-tracks to carry the 120 mm mortars in the weapons company, three Volkswagens, and a single three-ton truck. The battalion had 281 horses and seventy-four horse-drawn vehicles to move most of the battalion supplies and heavy weapons.

With very little motor transport available in the higher echelons, the infantry division could move on only foot or by rail. The men marched once they had been unloaded from trains that usually moved divisions long distances. Even if trucks were available for the men, the horses could be moved long distances only by rail. During offensives infantry divisions were required to march twelve miles or more per day, day after day, because no motor transport was available.

All of measures taken to provide additional men on the firing line were critical. By the fall of 1943 there were only a few divisions left in France with trained combat-fit men and enough horses and trucks to move their artillery and supplies. Most of the remaining divisions were either reserve divisions, made up of recruits in training, or occupation divisions of older men in fortifications with little transport.

Divisions being re-formed were shipped from France to Russia or Italy as soon as they reached a state of combat readiness. Hitler knew from deciphered scrambled transatlantic telephone conversations between Roosevelt and Churchill that the Western Allies had no intention of invading France in 1943 and that therefore he could use the troops in the East and South.

However, not all was well in the South. The invasion of Sicily in July had required immediate attention. The Germans fought a delaying action in Sicily while the troops in Italy were reinforced. The 1st Parachute Division formed in France from part of the 7th Flieger Division was sent to Sicily in July to reinforce the divisions already there.

To stabilize the situation in Italy Hitler sent the headquarters of the 2nd SS Panzer Corps and the Adolf Hitler SS Panzer Division from

Russia and four divisions from France to Italy. The divisions sent from France were Stalingrad divisions, including the 16th Panzer, which arrived in June; the 3rd and 29th Panzer Grenadier, which arrived in July; and the 26th Panzer, which arrived in August. By the end of July 1943, a semblance of a defense had been provided for Italy. The delaying action in Sicily cost the Germans few casualties and comparatively little equipment.

The next attack was expected in Sardinia, Corsica, Italy, or Greece, but there was little fear for the south of France until Sardinia and Corsica had been occupied. The guesswork ended on 25 July, when the Germans intercepted a telephone conversation between Churchill and Roosevelt that revealed that Italy would be invaded.

The knowledge that the Allies would invade Italy meant that there was no need to fear the invasion of France in 1943. Between May and August 1943 the Germans sent thirteen divisions into Italy, twelve from France and Belgium, and one from Denmark. Most of these units were still in the process of re-forming, but they did not anticipate immediate action. The units sent to Italy disarmed the Italian army after its surrender and fought a delaying action after the Allies landed.

The Germans had other demands that required resources. The Scandinavian countries were a source of divisions for other theaters during 1943. Denmark was a link in the communication to Norway and a potential landing site for the Allies. The total defensive force in Denmark was very weak in early 1943, but by October there were three divisional formations that were capable of defending the coast and preventing parachute landings. After transferring its recruits to the 179th Replacement Division, the 166th Replacement Division was sent to Denmark in January 1943. The 233d Reserve Panzer Division was formed on 10 August 1943 from the advanced training elements of the 233d Replacement Panzer Division in Germany. A new reserve division was sent to Denmark in September 1943. The 20th Luftwaffe Field Division, formed in Germany, was sent to Denmark in July 1943 and was still in the process of formation in October 1943. The 416th Infantry Division was formed in December 1941, with two regiments of Luftwaffe men and guard units, supported by only a single artillery battalion.

The Norway garrison was increased from eight divisions in June 1941 to twelve in April 1943 by combining the coastal defense battalions and coast artillery batteries into occupation divisions (230th, 270th, and 280th). These were divisions in name only. The 280th consisted of a headquarters, four fortress battalions, a signal company, and attached coast artillery.

Two divisions (199th and 702nd) guarded Narvik, the terminus of the rail line that brought Swedish iron ore to the Atlantic for shipment to Germany. Two additional divisions (14th Luftwaffe and 181st) held Trondheim, a major fishing port. Both of these ports had been occupied by the British in 1940. The 710th Division was stationed in Oslo, the political and economic center of the country; the 269th Division was east of Lillehammer; and the 214th Division was west of Oslo. The 25th Panzer and the 196th Divisions formed a reserve in the event that Sweden entered the war.

The infantry divisions in Norway provided regiments, battalions, and cadres for new occupation divisions in 1943. The 25th Panzer Division, formed in February 1942, had only one tank battalion (mostly Panzer IIs and French Somuas), three infantry battalions, and one artillery battalion. On 15 June 1943 the division was reinforced by training battalions and units from other divisions. Beginning in September 1943 there was a steady exodus of forces from Norway, which were replaced by newly formed occupation divisions, with older men.

When the 25th Panzer Division was shipped to France in August 1943, Panzer Division Norway was created, with three motorized infantry battalions, a tank battalion with thirty-six obsolete French tanks, an antitank battalion, and one artillery battalion. Before departure from Norway, the divisions were reinforced with young recruits, and the older men were transferred to occupation divisions.

Additional divisions were needed in the Balkans in 1943 to fight the partisans. Equipment for Josip Broz Tito's communists was supplied by British airdrops of German arms captured in North Africa. The well armed partisans caused the Germans increasing difficulty. In Croatia, fighting Tito, were the 714th, 717th, and 718th Infantry Divisions and the 187th Reserve, 7th SS Cavalry, and two Croatian divisions (369th and 373rd). Greece and Serbia were occupied by the 704th Infantry Division and three Bulgarian divisions. Eight Italian divisions completed the garrison in Albania and Greece. Holding Crete was necessary because it could have become an airbase. It was occupied by the Crete Fortress Brigade, later reinforced by the 11th Luftwaffe Division and the 22nd Infantry Division.

In April 1943 four occupation divisions were reorganized into jäger divisions (104th, 114th, 117th, and 118th) in the same way that I suggest could have been done in the spring of 1944. The older men were transferred to new fortress brigades and replaced with new recruits and recovered wounded from Germany.

The Balkans were reinforced with the 1st Mountain Division from Russia in May. In June 1943 two additional divisions came from France, the 1st Panzer Division was sent to Greece, and the 297th Infantry Division to Montenegro, on the Adriatic coast. By August the 100th Rifle Division (a rebuilt Stalingrad unit) had been added to the garrison. An additional reserve division (the 173rd) arrived along with the 11th SS Division, which was completing its training. The headquarters of the 2nd Panzer Army was sent from the Russian front to command the growing force.

By 25 July 1943 Hitler had increased the number of German divisions in the Balkans to twelve, including two on Crete. Army Group E in Yugoslavia had two German infantry divisions, two German reserve divisions, two Croatian divisions, four Bulgarian divisions, and two Hungarian divisions to fight Tito and his partisans.

By August 1943, the troops in the Balkans included eight Italian divisions, four Bulgarian divisions, two Croatian divisions, a Moslem SS division, the Prince Eugen SS Division (made up of *Volksdeutsch*), the Crete Brigade, and twelve German divisions (104th, 114th, 117th, 118th, 100th Jäger, 11th Air Force Field, 1st Mountain, 1st Panzer, 297th, 22nd, 173rd, and 187th).

The Balkans were proving to be a drain on German manpower. From a token force of five divisions in July 1942, the garrison grew to fifteen divisions on 1 July 1943 and to twenty-five by 1 June 1944. The partisans were holding down almost as many German divisions as the Allied armies in Italy. However, the Germans could not surrender the Balkans willingly in 1943. The Balkans were at the rear of the line of communications of the Army Group South in Russia as well as adjacent to the northern entry into Italy.

The quality of the German army in France declined during 1943. The defense of France was in the hands of the occupation divisions, assigned permanently to coastal sectors. They were familiar with their areas, and, installed in permanent defenses, they could defend the beaches in the most economical way in terms of equipment and manpower. Most of the officers and men were overage, and there were fewer weapons than in other divisions. A large proportion of the weapons were French, Polish, and Yugoslav, firing different kinds of ammunition. Most of the occupation divisions had only two infantry regiments and two field artillery battalions, plus a medium artillery battalion. All of the artillery was horse drawn. The divisions were spread very thin; there were only three to cover 300 miles south of the Loire River.

Reserve divisions also reinforced the occupation forces. The reserve divisions were comprised of advanced training battalions. In a German program instituted in 1943, training battalions in Germany were divided into two parts. One battalion remained in Germany as a replacement battalion, providing basic training and holding recuperating wounded; the new battalion was given the designation of "reserve battalion" and received new recruits who had completed basic training. Most of these new reserve battalions were shipped to France for occupation duties and were assembled into reserve divisions. As the men completed their training, they were sent to Russia as replacements. By the end of 1943, some reserve divisions were no longer needed, because the training period had been shortened and the replacements were sent directly from Germany to divisions on the Russian front or in France.

Some of the reserve divisions were manning the coastal sectors along with the occupation divisions. In July 1943 three reserve divisions were on coastal sectors, and more were proposed for this assignment. All of the reserve divisions were ordered to form combat groups, with officers, noncoms, vehicles, and trained soldiers. The divisions also formed alarm battalions to defend against parachute landings. Two reserve panzer divisions (155th and 179th), each reinforced with an artillery replacement battalion and an engineer company, were sent to France as a mobile reserve in early August 1943.

On 25 July 1943 Hitler issued an order to build up the army in France and the Low Countries. In July 1943, twenty-five occupation divisions and one reserve division guarded the coast; six infantry divisions and two motorized divisions were in reserve behind the coast; and nine reserve divisions were training in the countryside. A Bosnian SS division was also training in France. A little improvement was seen by 6 September 1943, when the German army in France included twenty-seven infantry and occupation divisions, six panzer and motorized divisions, and seven reserve divisions. However, many of the divisions had suffered heavy losses in Russia and had been sent back to France to refit. As soon as divisions were rehabilitated, they were sent to Italy or back to Russia. France was a source of fresh divisions for the East until November 1943.

On 28 October 1943 the German army in the West had twenty-three divisions on the coast and twenty-three in reserve. Of those on the coast, seventeen were occupation divisions, five were capable only of defense, and one was mobile. Each division had one or more Ost battalions, combat units made up of Russian prisoners. All of the occupation divisions used captured French, Russian, and other foreign weapons. Of the twenty-three divisions forming the mobile reserve, two had not arrived, and eleven were new divisions being formed. The total ration strength of the forces in the West was 1,370,000 in the army, navy, and Luftwaffe, plus service troops and hiwis, for a total of 1,709,000.

By November 1943 the overall position had stabilized. The Germans gave ground grudgingly in Italy and held on the Dnieper River in the East. The multiple Soviet operations began after Kursk were halted with the arrival of a new group of fresh German divisions from France. These new divisions helped stop the Russians at Kiev in October 1943 in a series of bloody battles. However, on 3 November the Soviets launched a massive attack north of Kiev, broke the Dnieper River defense line, and captured Kiev. A new crisis was at hand, and there were no reserves available.

However, in late 1943 the Allied leaders met in Yalta and agreed to delay the second front until June 1944, giving Hitler a window of opportunity—he could strip the West of divisions, as long as he replaced them by June 1944. On the same day the Red Army opened its offensive at Kiev, Hitler issued an edict to form new armies in the West to oppose the second front expected in June 1944. Meanwhile no more new divisions would be sent to the Russian front from France.

On 3 November 1943 Directive Number 51, the order to rebuild the army in France, placed the West in top priority for the first time. The crucial point in Directive 51 was that although there still remained considerable space in Russia for strategic withdrawal and rearguard actions, an Allied landing would place the enemy right at Germany's throat, the Ruhr industrial section. The objective of the directive was to create a force that would defeat the anticipated invasion.

Under the new directive the panzer and panzer grenadier divisions in the West were reinforced and received new equipment. Each occupation division was to receive about a thousand additional machine guns. The 20th Luftwaffe, 12th SS Panzer Grenadier, and 21st Panzer were given additional men and weapons. The reserve divisions were to be filled with recruits. This was a weak program, however, far from enough to withstand an invasion of France. Few new divisions were formed after November 1943.

To implement a more meaningful program, Hitler issued another directive. On 27 November 1943 he announced a plan for the army and the SS to produce a million new combat soldiers. The plan reduced the service elements in the table of organization of divisions by 25 percent and abolished some independent service and headquarters organizations. The goal was to save 560,000 men: 120,000 from 150 infantry divisions, 20,000 from panzer and panzer grenadier divisions, 120,000 from service units, 260,000 through substituting Russian volunteers for German troops in service units, 20,000 from headquarters, and an additional 20,000 from miscellaneous sources. Special control commissions were organized to visit units to ensure that the cuts were made.

Under the order, many men previously considered unfit for duty were reclassified as fit for limited service. These limited-service men replaced combat-fit men in service, communications, and headquarters units. Those with stomach disorders were formed into battalions and even into a combat division that received special food—stationed in Denmark, where dairy products were readily available. Deaf men were formed into "ear battalions" and assigned to defensive positions. In addition to transferring men from the rear echelon, navy and air force men were sent to the army. The result was a great increase in available men to build new divisions. Fortunately, most of them remained in the Replacement Army until after July 1944, and few new divisions were created before June 1944.

To supplement German manpower, the army recruited an additional 300,000 hiwis and men previously exempt because of their doubtful loyalty to Germany. *Volksdeutsch*, men born outside of Germany with one or two German parents, were subject to conscription, but were classified, as we have seen, according to their degree of loyalty to Germany and their political attitude. List I were active Nazis. List II were passive Nazis who had preserved their allegiance to Germany. Men in Lists I and II obviously would make politically reliable soldiers and did not need special treatment.

Most of the *Volksdeutsch* were from the Polish corridor, territory taken from Germany at the end of World War I. List III were racial Germans who had absorbed Polish ways but were considered susceptible to conversion to Nazi ideology. The men were given ten-year probationary citizenships and drafted but were subjected to special rules; for instance, they could not be promoted above the rank equal to an American private first class. By 1 April 1944, 77,861 *Volksdeutsch* of List III were in the army.

In addition, there was a List IV, men hostile to Germany, who were not drafted into the army at all. As manpower needs grew however, the army designated as List III and drafted some men previously considered antagonistic to Germany. I talked with a veteran who had been born in Luxembourg but was working in a theater in Berlin in early 1944. He had been classified as a List IV but in the spring of 1944 was reclassified, inducted, given four days' training, and sent to an artillery unit in France. Many of these reclassified men deserted at the first opportunity, as did the veteran I interviewed. A former staff officer in the Polish army in Italy told me that he regularly visited the prisoner of war camps to obtain replacements for the Polish divisions that fought in Italy and France.

The number of hiwis increased steadily. The new-type division of late 1943 increased the authorized strength of hiwis from 700 to 2,005, although not all divisions had full allotments. The Germans also initiated aggressive recruiting among Soviets in the prisoner of war camps, and by June 1944, 200 Ost battalions had been formed. Given the option of dying of starvation and ill treatment, many Soviet prisoners volunteered, especially members of dissident minorities. The Ost battalions were not used in Russia; they were sent to France and Italy in exchange for German battalions sent to reinforce divisions in Russia, two Ost battalions for one German. Sending the Ost battalions to France and Italy also made desertion more difficult. Specific instructions were given regarding the use of these troops; they were to be employed only when supported by German units, even though that plan prevented the release of larger numbers of German battalions. Discipline was to be maintained by the severest methods.

During the summer of 1943 ten battalions of Ost troops had been sent to France without weapons. They were armed with French rifles and machine guns. In September a further 15,800 Ost troops were sent, and during November and December another 25,000 were exchanged for German troops in the West, including Norway and Denmark. Between September and December 1943 sixty Ost battalions were exchanged for thirty German infantry battalions, which were sent to the East to reinforce weak German units. For example, on 22 October 1943 a battalion of the 319th Division, which formed the garrison of the Channel Islands, was sent to Russia, where it became the II Battalion, 122nd Infantry Regiment, 50th Infantry Division. To replace this battalion, the 319th Division received the 643rd Ost Battalion and the 823rd Georgian Battalion.

By the end of 1943, the Germans had enrolled 370,000 Ost troops and were using 130,000 hiwis in service units. The foreigners helped to spread German manpower and permit its use in the most essential roles. Nevertheless, the Germans did not deceive themselves concerning the combat value of these troops.

Pending the collection of additional manpower as a result of the November 1943 plan, the Germans adopted a temporary program in Russia by which the remnants of two or three divisions were combined to form a division-sized unit called a "corps detachment" (*corps abteilungen*). The corps detachment was a makeshift to utilize the surviving units of badly mauled divisions. Rather than send these burned-out divisions to France at a time when the Germans were trying to stem the Soviet advance, about a third of the men remained in Russia in the corps detachments under the assumption that when replacements were available, the detachments would be restored to full divisions. The men became available in the spring of 1944, but these divisions were not reconstituted.

Meanwhile the headquarters, service, and support units of the wrecked divisions were to form new divisions in France. One division provided the corps detachment with headquarters, service, and support troops. The other two divisions formed "division groups," equal to infantry regiments. The headquarters and service elements of two divisions and six regiments were sent to France and rebuilt as new divisions with new numbers but the same replacement battalions.

The first corps detachments were formed during November 1943 from remnants of divisions that had suffered heavy losses in the summer and fall of 1943. Six corps detachments were formed, A through F, the first five by Army Groups South and Center and the last in March 1944 by Army Group South Ukraine. The typical organization included three regiment-sized groups, each representing a former division and receiving replacements from the replacement battalion that had served the former division. The regiment groups usually consisted of two battalions, each representing regiments of a former division. In this way, the normal course of replacement continued, with men from a given military district and replacement battalion going to a unit representing the division.

Corps Detachment D was formed by the 9th German Army in December 1943 from the 56th and 262nd Infantry Divisions. The corps detachment was assigned to the 9th Corps of the 3rd Panzer Army on 23 June 1944. Corps Detachment D had the 171st and 234th Regiments from the 56th Division, and Division Group 262 representing the 262nd Division, with the 462nd and 482nd Regiment Groups, equal to battalions, representing two regiments of the former 262nd Division. Corps Detachment D was abolished in July 1944, after suffering heavy losses in the battle for White Russia. In late July 1944 when the logjam in the Replacement Army was removed, the 56th Infantry Division was re-formed from part of the corps detachment, and the remainder was used in the creation of the 277th Infantry Division.

In addition to division groups in the corps detachments, from September 1943 to May 1944 infantry remnants of sixteen divisions were reduced to division groups and attached to other infantry divisions in place of infantry regiments. In this way, a division that had enough men to form two infantry regiments would receive the equivalent of a third regiment in the form of a division group and thus have the authorized seven-battalion organization. Of the sixteen divisions thus used, nine provided the noninfantry components of new divisions created in France, Italy, and the Balkans. The divisional headquarters, artillery regiment, engineer battalion, signal battalion, supply units, and other components were sent from Russia and given new numbers. Six were formed in France (352nd, 271st, 276th, 273rd, 272nd, and 353rd), the 362nd in Italy, the 367th in the Balkans, and the 357th by the Replacement Army in Radom, Poland.

The intent had been that once the crisis had passed, the normal flow of replacements would permit the regimental groups to be reinforced to full divisions. The creation of thirty new divisions beginning in September 1943 in the Twenty-first, Twenty-second, Twenty-third, and Twenty-fifth Waves placed an unusual demand on the supply of replacements. However, the million-man program did provide more than enough men within a few months.

On 15 October 1943 the Germans began formation of the Twenty-first Wave, with nine new-type divisions (349th, 352nd, 353rd, 357th, 359th, 361st, 362nd, 363rd, and 367th). Each division used the headquarters and service elements of a worn-out division (217th, 321st, 328th, 327th, 293rd, 86th, 268th, 339th, and 330th), most of which had become division groups in the corps detachments in Russia. The new divisions were formed in France (three), Denmark (two), Poland (two), Italy (one), and Croatia (one). For example the 352nd Division replaced the 321st Division. Other elements of the 352nd came

from the 137th, 254th, 356th, 371st, and 389th Divisions, the 3rd
Flak Company of the Antitank Replacement Battalion, and the Assault
Gun Replacement Battalion.

The Twenty-first Wave was well equipped with artillery, machine
guns, and twenty-four self-propelled guns. The men came from the
class of 1926 (aged seventeen) and others from the Replacement Army
ranging from twenty to forty-two years of age, men previously classified as unfit for combat from the classes of 1901 through 1922. The
formations were complete by February 1944.

The creation of the Twenty-second Wave (271st, 272rd, 275th,
276th, 277th, and 278th Divisions) was ordered on 23 October 1943
under the same conditions as the Twenty-first Wave (see Table 4.1).
The six divisions of the Twenty-second Wave were created in January
1944; five were formed in France and one in Italy. The division cadres came from burned-out divisions from Russia (113th, 216th, 223rd,
38th, 262nd, and 335th). From two to four battalions of recruits for
each division came from six reserve divisions and from training battalions. The 271st received its cadre from the 113th Division and
additional men from the 102nd, 129th, 137th, 294, 304, and 356
Divisions. Each of the reserve battalions formed a new infantry battalion in the new division.

In January 1944 the Twenty-third Wave was assembled from four
field training divisions formed from the remnants of four training divisions of the same number. The process was not continued; creation
of new field divisions stopped abruptly.

Table 4.1
The 22nd Wave

Division	Cadre	Other Cadre	Replacement Division
271	113	102, 129, 137, 294, 304, 356	
272	216	371	182, 189
275	223	94, 102, 255	158
276	38	52, 137, 332	157, 189
277	262	26, 71, 137	141, 187
278	333	110, 137, 161	

The *Schatten,* or shadow, divisions were a means of keeping control of new units in the Replacement Army rather than release them to the field army. Their table of organization, three rifle regiments and a few support units, was ideally suited for internal security duty. The Twenty-fourth Wave consisted of three *Schatten* divisions bearing the names of training camps formed in January 1944 by the staffs of reserve divisions. Supposedly these divisions would be used to flesh out the remnants of burned-out divisions that had sustained heavy losses in riflemen but few in headquarters, service, or artillery units. However, there were divisions in Russia that needed these battalions without the intermediate step of forming the *Schatten* division.

The order of 12 December 1943 anticipated the completion of the Twenty-fourth Wave by 15 March 1944. The cadres came from reserve divisions, and the men came from the classes of 1925 and 1926 (eighteen and nineteen-year-olds). The 141st Reserve Division formed Division Demba; the 151st Reserve Division formed Division Mielau; and the 173rd Reserve Division formed Division Milowitz. In March 1944 the three divisions rebuilt the 214th, 389th, and 331st Infantry Divisions. The formation of the *Schatten* divisions was a clear indication that manpower was available to create new divisions.

The Twenty-fifth Wave was formed from the reinforced infantry regiments created in late 1943 to defend the West. These regiments came from elements of the Replacement Army. In January and February 1944 these regiments were combined with the remnants of divisions burned out in the East to form six new divisions (77th, 84th, 85th, 89th, 91st, and 92nd). The divisions were combat ready by May 15, 1944, organized as "Type 1944" infantry divisions. These divisions had two regiments of three battalions each, a fusilier battalion, three artillery battalions, an engineer battalion, and a field replacement battalion. Three of the divisions were formed in France, one in Norway, one in Italy, and one in Germany. The 91st Division played a major role in the defense of Normandy and was considered first-rate by the Americans.

The Twenty-sixth Wave included four new *Schatten* divisions created in April 1944 and used to rebuild the 198th, 34th, 65th, and 715th Infantry Divisions in June 1944; also, one regiment of Division Ostpreussen went to the 75th Infantry Division. The new divisions had two infantry regiments each of three battalions, a single artillery battalion with eight light and four heavy howitzers, a motorized anti-tank company, and an engineer battalion with two companies. The

Schatten divisions had few service elements, because few casualties occurred in those units. The rebuilding process was completed by August 1944.

No other divisions were formed until August 1944, as the Replacement Army held back troops from the front. Between January and June 1944 only four *Schatten* divisions of the Twenty-sixth Wave were formed by the Replacement Army from reserve divisions in France, and even these were withheld from the front until June, when they were used to rebuild four depleted divisions.

An example of the use of a *Schatten* division was Division Mielau, used to rebuild the 214th Infantry Division. The 1st Regiment headquarters became the headquarters of the new 568th Regiment of the 214th Division. Elements of the 1st Battalion of the 1st Regiment of Division Mielau reinforced the existing 355th and 367th Regiments of the 214th Division. The II Battalion became the I Battalion, 568th Regiment; the III Battalion became the II Battalion, 568th Regiment; and antitank and cannon companies of the 1st Regiment assumed the same roles in the new 568th Regiment. The headquarters of the 2nd Regiment became a coast defense headquarters for Army Detachment Narva; the I Battalion of the 2nd Regiment became the Fusilier Battalion of the 214th Division; the II Battalion was used for replacements for the 11th Infantry Division; and the III Battalion was used for replacements for the 61st Infantry Division. The Mielau Artillery Battalion became the I Battalion, 214th Artillery Regiment; the Mielau Panzer Jäger Company became the Assault Gun Battalion for the 121st Infantry Division; and elements of the Mielau Engineer Battalion were divided among the 12th Engineer Battalion of the 12th Air Force Division, the 214th Division Engineer Battalion, and the 121st Division Engineer Battalion. As a result, one division was completely rebuilt, and two divisions received significant reinforcements.

In addition to the infantry divisions formed in waves, ten occupation divisions were created and assigned to the West between July 1943 and January 1944 (47th, 48th, 49th, 70th, 242nd, 243rd, 244th, 245th, 265th, 266th). Four burned-out panzer divisions came from the East (2nd, 9th, 11th, and 19th), and two new panzer divisions (116th and Lehr) were formed. The 116th Panzer was rebuilt from the burned-out 16th Panzer Grenadier Division and the 179th Reserve Panzer Division. Panzer Lehr was assembled from school troops. The 1st and 2nd SS Panzer Divisions came from the East in April and May 1944. Two new parachute divisions were formed in the

West, and one from the East was rebuilt. The weak Norway Panzer Division was created from tank units stationed in Norway.

Also not part of the wave structure were twelve divisions formed between August 1943 and March 1944, including the three panzer divisions mentioned above. The divisions were formed by redesignating existing units or gathering foreign volunteers into divisions. The 42nd Jäger Division was created from the 187th Reserve Division. The 133rd Fortress Division was merely a change in name for the Crete Fortress Brigade, not a new formation. The 41st Fortress Division was formed for occupation duty in the Balkans in February 1944. Three divisions of non-Germans were formed—the 392nd Croatian Division, the 162nd Turkoman Division (from Turkish ethnic groups in the Caucasus), and the 1st Cossack Cavalry Division. The Croats went to Russia; the Turks were used in Italy; and the Cossacks fought Tito's partisans in Yugoslavia.

The Rhodes Assault Division was simply a new title for the occupation forces on the island of Rhodes in the Mediterranean. The 1st Ski Jäger Division was created from the Ski Jäger Brigade in Russia in January 1944. The 18th Artillery Division, created from the 18th Panzer Division's survivors, included nine artillery battalions, an antiaircraft battalion, and an assault gun battery with ten guns (this experimental artillery division was abolished in April 1944). Table 4.2 lists the twelve newly designated divisions.

In addition, the Germans reorganized seven divisions in France as occupation divisions, including the 319th, 708th, 709th, 711th, 712th, 716th, and 719th. These divisions formed much of the coastal defense force in northern France in June 1944.

In July 1943, while the successful program to strengthen the army in the West in late 1943 was taking place, the conspiracy to assassinate Hitler and use the Replacement Army to gain control of Germany began to take form. The plotters intended to withhold replacements and delay the formation of new divisions in early 1944 in order to have the maximum number of troops in the Replacement Army when the assassination took place.

The conspirators planned to utilize the *Valkure* program, which was originated to provide reinforcements for the field army from the Replacement Army in the event of a crisis. The *Valkure* plan was devised in the summer of 1941 by Gen. Erich Fromm, commander of the Replacement Army. It called for the formation of units using the cadre, convalescents able to fight, and the partially trained new recruits in

Table 4.2
New Divisions, August 1943 to May 1944

Division	Cadre	Date
42nd Jäger	187th Reserve Division	February 1944
133rd Fortress	Crete Fortress Brigade	January 1944
41st Fortress	39th Infantry Division	December 1943
392nd Croatian	Croatian regiments	October 1943
162nd Turkoman	162nd Division elements	August 1943
1st Cossack	Pannowitz Cavalry unit	August 1943
Norway Panzer	21st Panzer Brigade	October 1943
Rhodes Assault	22nd Division and Crete Fortress Division	May 1943
116th Panzer	16th Panzer and 179th Reserve Panzer Divisions	March 1944
Panzer Lehr	School troops	January 1944
18th Artillery	18th Panzer Division	October 1943
1st Ski Jäger	Ski Jäger Brigade	August 1943

the Replacement Army. *Valkure* units were used to rebuild the German army in December 1941 and again in July 1942.

In 1943 the conspirators altered their plan to use the Replacement Army to establish control of Germany after the assassination. Previous plans to use the Replacement Army as part of the coup had been unsuccessful, because Fromm would not cooperate. The new variation assumed that at the last moment Fromm would be compelled to participate and issue the necessary orders or would be replaced. However, the conspirators realized that detailed plans had to be made to ensure that replacement units all around Germany would know what to do and would respond immediately and without question.

On 31 July 1943 General Fromm issued a top secret order to the commanders of the military districts to form combat units from the replacement battalions in their districts. The new facet of this order was that *Valkure* units were to be ready not only to reinforce the field army but also to suppress internal disturbances caused by saboteurs or uprisings by foreign laborers and prisoners in Germany. The district commanders were ordered to complete the organization of these combat units and carry out exercises by 12 August 1943.

The impetus for the secret order for the mobilization of Replacement Army units was the series of air raids on Hamburg, which began on 25 July 1943 and ended on 30 July 1943. The six continuous days and nights of bombing by the U.S. Air Force and the RAF destroyed a large portion of the city. Military units had been called into the city to maintain order and restore some semblance of normal functioning. The catastrophe was so serious that the German leadership feared if it was repeated, civil government would collapse. Clearing the debris and finding the dead was accomplished by the use of prisoners and the local Replacement Army units. From that experience, Hitler realized the need to have a plan to mobilize the local replacement units in a matter of hours—thus the new *Valkure* units, which were to be formed into reinforced battalions from all elements of the Replacement Army. The order for *Valkure* Stage I required that all company-sized units be combat ready in six hours. *Valkure* Stage II required that these companies be formed into battalions and combat groups as soon as possible. The combat groups were assigned signal, transport, and other administrative personnel to prepare them for combat.

On 6 October 1943 an additional order required that all units of the field army in Germany that were re-forming were to become part of the *Valkure* organization, under the command of General Fromm. On 11 February 1944 a further order outlined the formation of regiments and their assignment to vital points in their area. The regiments included two or three infantry battalions, an infantry gun company, one or two antitank companies, two or three artillery batteries, and an engineer company. These regiments were to be available where needed and could be ordered up individually, making them very flexible tools in the hands of the conspirators.

The *Valkure* orders remained top secret, and few individuals were aware of the plan. As no Nazi Party or SS organizations were included in the *Valkure* plan, the conspirators could call up a military force without the knowledge of the Nazi Party. The problem was that General Fromm personally had to issue the code words to the various military districts, but as noted, the plotters believed that if Hitler were assassinated Fromm would cooperate.

Officers willing to collaborate with the conspirators were placed in strategic posts in military districts throughout Germany. The organization was not complete, and some officers transferred later could not be replaced. To supplant people already in positions, the conspirators selected for each military district liaison officers who would be available to carry through the mobilization plan. The plan was so advanced that rehearsals were possible, under various disguises; for example, in Berlin the troops were rehearsed on the excuse that civil government might collapse as a result of heavy air bombing, as had occurred in Hamburg in July 1943. In November 1943 a rehearsal was held in Berlin that placed armored and infantry battalions in the center of Berlin in one hour.

In the winter of 1943, to ensure that there would be ample trained men available, the Replacement Army reduced the flow of replacements to the field army. The explanation given was that because the fear of an immediate Allied invasion had ended with the attack on Italy, there was no need to rush replacements to the West. The rate of loss on the Eastern Front declined after January 1944, and only a few replacements were needed. New recruits were kept in Germany beyond their training period rather than being sent to training divisions in France or to Russia.

The objective of the generals was to negotiate with the Western Allies while Germany was still a powerful force. Only under that condition was there any possibility of obtaining a settlement favorable to Germany. By the end of 1943, the war had once again turned to Germany's favor. The British were not eager to invade Europe and repeat the bloodbath of World War I. American interest was divided between Europe and Asia. The conspirators accordingly had good reason to believe that once Hitler was removed they would have bargaining power to make peace. Neither the British nor the Americans relished the thought of the removal of Germany and creation of a power vacuum in Central Europe that Joseph Stalin would be eager to fill.

Germany's war potential was far greater at the end of 1943 than at the beginning of the year. After the heavy losses in January 1943, the rate remained below 100,000 per month, which could be sustained by the Replacement Army. In six months the losses were fewer than 60,000, fewer than 150 men each for the more than 500 replacement battalions in Germany (see Table 4.3).

In November 1943, as noted, the decision at Yalta to launch the second front in June 1944 forced Hitler to build a new army in France; his edict of 3 November 1943 giving top priority to reinforcing France provided a cover for the Replacement Army program of denying the German army in Russia of fresh divisions to withstand future Red

Table 4.3
Permanent Losses in 1943

Month	Killed	Missing	Total
January 1943	37,000	127,595	164,596
February 1943	42,000	15,500	57,500
March 1943	38,115	5,208	43,323
April 1943	15,300	3,500	18,800
May 1943	16,200	74,500	90,700
June 1943	13,400	1,300	14,700
July 1943	57,800	18,300	76,100
August 1943	58,000	26,400	84,400
September 1943	48,788	21,923	70,711
October 1943	47,036	16,783	63,819
November 1943	40,167	17,886	58,054
December 1943	35,290	14,712	50,002

Army offensives. Many divisions in France had been transferred to Italy or Russia by November 1943, but more would be needed. If no additional reserves were available, the Soviet drives would stop only when the Russians outran their supply system and had to await the repair of railroads. Cutting off the flow of combat replacement battalions to the East prevented the commanders in the Russia from reconstituting the division groups in thirty-two complete divisions as had been planned. To make matters worse, the conspirators not only choked off reserves for the East but prevented the formation of enough new divisions to hold France.

The November demand for 1,000,000 men for the front had been met, but most of the men were held back by the Replacement Army. The Replacement Army had provided 968,500 men for new units and replacements in old units in the last six months of 1943, but the number of men released in the first half of 1944 dwindled to a trickle. Had the Replacement Army fulfilled its obligations in early 1944, an additional sixty divisions could have provided both the East and West with a strategic reserve that would have prolonged the war for at least a year.

5

Calm before the Storm, February 1944 to June 1944

Even though 1943 was disastrous for the Germans, matters smoothed out for a time early in 1944 before the Allied invasion of France and the Russian offensive in White Russia. The Russians had paused in early 1944, perhaps to watch the development of the Allied invasion.

From August 1943 to January 1944 the Germans suffered a series of disasters on the Eastern Front. The loss of troops was appalling. From July to October 1943 the losses in the East were 911,000 killed, wounded, and captured, but only 421,000 replacements were provided, a net loss of 489,000. The total number of men on the Eastern Front dropped from 3,138,000 on 1 July 1943, before the attack on Kursk, to 2,619,000 on 1 December 1943.

From November 1943 to February 1944, 646,000 men were lost, and only 460,000 were replaced, for a net loss of 184,000. In sharp contrast to the disparity of the earlier period, in the three months between March 1944 and May 1944 only 342,000 German soldiers were lost in the East, while 357,000 replacements arrived, a net gain of 16,000. This was a paltry amount considering the staggering number of trained combat replacement battalions in Germany. The total number of replacements was 100,000 fewer than in the previous three

Table 5.1
Number of Divisions in the German Army

	Army	SS	Luftwaffe	Total
1 July 1943	243	11	22	276
1 July 1944	257	21	6	284

months. These figures were a clear indication that more could have been done to replace the losses of previous months and to rebuild the division groups.

The German army had only six additional divisions in June 1944 than in July 1943, despite Hitler's order to send an additional million men to the front and the potential in the Replacement Army for creating sixty more divisions. The total divisions in the German army included forming, security, and reserve divisions. The major shift was 1944 was the elimination of most of the Luftwaffe field divisions and the formation of additional SS divisions (see Table 5.1).

From August 1943 to May 1944, only fifty-four new German divisions were formed—thirty-seven army, three parachute, and thirteen SS divisions. Included in the thirty-seven new army divisions were eight occupation divisions, twenty infantry divisions, three divisions of non-Germans, three panzer divisions, and three special divisions. The three special divisions were the 1st Ski Jäger Division, the Rhodes Assault Division, and the 18th Artillery Division.

The rebuilding program began in France in September 1943, with the creation of eight occupation divisions. Four of the occupation divisions (47th, 48th, 49th, and 70th) were formed from the 156th, 171st, 191st, and 165th Reserve Divisions by December 1943. The reserve divisions were made up of battalions of new recruits receiving advanced infantry training in France.

The new SS divisions included five panzer grenadier, six divisions of non-Germans, and two panzer grenadier brigades. The three parachute divisions were elite infantry divisions raised by the Luftwaffe, but they were not trained parachutists. These divisions were not the same as the small Luftwaffe divisions formed in 1942. Eight Luftwaffe divisions were abolished between January and May 1944. Four were used to provide replacements for the 4th, 5th, 6th, and 12th Luftwaffe

Divisions, which became part of the army; the remaining four provided replacements for the 28th Jäger, 304th, 76th, 126th, 225th, and 170th Infantry Divisions.

The formation of the fifty-four new divisions was offset by the loss of forty-one divisions in Russia between July 1943 and May 1944, most as a result of combat losses. Most of the burned-out divisions were rebuilt in France as new divisions in 1943 and early 1944. The new divisions enabled the Germans to stabilize the fronts in both Italy and Russia by November 1943. In Italy the Germans were able to contain the Allied advance by a very skillful rear-guard action that ended in a stalemate at Cassino during the winter of 1943. Also ending in a stalemate was the Allied attempt to bypass Cassino by means of an amphibious attack at Anzio. The Germans held their ground in Italy from the spring of 1944 until the drive that gave Rome to the Americans in June 1944.

In the last three months of 1943, twenty-three divisions were lost in Russia. The Russians were comparatively quiet for the first six months of 1944, at least in the north and center. Two divisions were lost in the Crimea (111th and 336th), and many more were battered in the Soviet advance in the Ukraine during the spring. As usual, operations on the Russian front halted when the spring thaw made the roads impassable. After February 1944 the Germans lost comparatively few divisions on the Russian front, until June.

During 1944, the German armed forces reached their peak strength of 12,070,000, including the army, Replacement Army, air force, navy, SS, foreign forces, and civilian workers. However, a relatively small percentage of the army was in combat on 1 June 1944. The Replacement Army continued to hold 600,000 men in replacement battalions, training divisions, and *Schatten* divisions. There were 2.5 million men in the Replacement Army. In the first six months of 1944, the Replacement Army provided 449,500 new replacements for combat divisions and returned 356,500 wounded to their divisions. In addition, 63,000 men were used to refit burned-out divisions, and 261,000 men went to newly organized divisions, a total of 1,130,000 men. The vast majority became replacements for existing divisions. As detailed in Table 5.2, the field army in Russia increased by 224,000 men in the month of June, when losses were negligible.

The 2.5 million men in the Replacement Army in July 1944 included 1,330,000 assigned to the training function, 500,000 new inductees in training, 230,000 cadre and men in schools, 200,000

Table 5.2
Increase in Strength of Army Groups in Russia

Army Group	1 May 1944	1 June 1944
South Ukraine	360,984	418,197
North Ukraine	423,579	475,347
Center	499,450	578,225
North	340,958	376,268
Total	1,624,971	1,848,037

recovering wounded in replacement battalions, and 400,000 men in march battalions ready to go to the front. The remainder of the Replacement Army included 700,000 men in hospitals, 300,000 guards for installations and prisoners, and 170,000 hospital workers.

Clearly, something was amiss when there were 400,000 fully trained men, equal to an army group, waiting in camps in the Replacement Army. Given the impending crisis in the summer of 1944, the 400,000 men in the trained march battalions and at least 200,000 of the recovering wounded in the Replacement Army could well have been used to form new divisions.

The Russian desire to await the Allied attack in France before launching the next drive gave the Germans a respite in the East until June 1944. The slower tempo of operations enabled the Germans to rebuild their divisions in the north and center with recruits and returning wounded. However, German army obligations were increasing with the need to form an army to defend France. In early 1944 the German army should have been creating new divisions to replace those destroyed on the Russian front and to reinforce the army groups in France. Instead, burned-out divisions from the East were sent to France and not returned as in previous years. The new divisions remained in France or were sent to other theaters. In sharp contrast to previous years, no fresh divisions were sent to Russia in the spring of 1944 to provide an operational reserve.

Table 5.3 shows the dramatic shift of forces from the Eastern Front to France, Italy, and the Balkans between July 1943 and June 1944. The net loss of the thirty German divisions in Russia was offset by small increases elsewhere. The German army in 1943–1944 was pri-

Table 5.3
Allocation of German Divisions

Theater	July 1943	June 1944
Russia	187	157
Finland	7	7
Norway	14	12
Denmark	3	3
West (France and Low Countries)	44	54
Italy	7	27
Balkans	15	25
Total	277	285

marily focused on improving their defensive position in the West and maintaining a balance in the Balkans and Italy. While the Russian front was losing thirty divisions, twenty were sent to Italy, ten were added to France, and ten were sent to the Balkans.

The losses on the Russian front in the face of a growing Red Army would lead to disaster in June 1944. In contrast to the shrinking forces in the East, the Germans added ten divisions to oppose the second front in the summer of 1944. The paltry increase in France was far from enough to forestall a similar catastrophe in the West. Italy and the Balkans remained running sores, receiving reinforcements adequate only to continue the battles of attrition. The most astonishing fact in Table 5.3 is that the total number of divisions increased by only eight, despite Hitler's order for an all-out mobilization and the addition of 1,000,000 men at the front.

Instead of replacing losses in the divisions in Russia, remnants of divisions were either combined into corps detachments or sent to the West, where they were used to form new divisions. Many of the abolished divisions were reduced to division groups and assigned to corps detachments or used to add third regiments to weakened division. The remnant of the 82nd Division, for instance, was used to fill out the 254th Division in May 1944.

The staffs of the abolished divisions were sometimes used to form new divisions. The 18th Panzer Division, abolished in October 1943, was rebuilt as an artillery division in April 1944. The 16th Panzer

Grenadier Division was destroyed in March 1944, and the remnant was sent to France to create the new 116th Panzer Division.

Not only was the number of divisions reduced, but the divisions themselves were made smaller. In the fall of 1943, as noted above, the German army had revised the table of organization of an infantry division with the designation Infantry Division, N.A. (new type), with 13,656 men. On 10 January 1944 the table of organization of the infantry division was reduced. The new division—Infantry Division, New Type (Reduced)—still had six infantry battalions and a fusilier battalion. Anticipating a shortage of replacements, the Germans placed increased reliance on heavy weapons, rather than riflemen (which were reduced to a bare minimum), to provide firepower. The objectives of the new organization were to maintain the number of infantry, as well as to increase the number of weapons, reduce the service components, replace light trucks with vehicles better suited to the Eastern Front, and improve the ratio between support troops and combat troops.

Among the savings in German manpower was the substitution of trucks and small tracked vehicles for the horses that pulled the artillery and wagons. Another saving in the reduced division was the decrease by 60 percent in the amount of ammunition held by the division as a basic reserve, eliminating 231 men, 336 horses, and twenty trucks. The rationale for the cut in munitions was that attacking divisions would receive assistance in supplying munitions from army troops, while divisions in defensive sectors would have ample opportunity to obtain the reduced amount of munitions from army depots. The total saving in the smaller division was 1,261 men, reducing the total German division to an authorized strength of 12,395, including 1,455 hiwi service troops and 9,652 German combat soldiers.

The reduced German infantry division of 1944 included three grenadier regiments, each with a headquarters company; an infantry gun company (two heavy 105 mm howitzers and six light 75 mm infantry guns); an antitank company with three 75 mm antitank guns and thirty-six antitank rocket launchers; and two grenadier battalions, each with four companies with six heavy machine guns, four heavy mortars, and six medium mortars. The division also included an artillery regiment with thirty-six 105 mm howitzers and nine (later twelve) 150 mm howitzers, a fusilier battalion, an engineer battalion, and an antitank battalion with twelve either 75 mm or 50 mm antitank guns. Some divisions also had ten assault guns and either nine 37 mm antiaircraft guns or twelve 20 mm antiaircraft guns. The infantry regiment had an authorized strength of 1,987 men and the fusilier battalion 708, with about 150 men in each of the rifle companies. Usually the battalions had only 500 men, with 100 in each of the three rifle companies and the machine-gun company.

Although German infantry divisions had suffered from attrition and lack of replacements in the past, there was no shortage of men or weapons in early 1944. The result was overstrength divisions composed of battle-hardened veterans and well trained replacements. An important factor in the improvement of German divisions on the Russian front in the first six months of 1944 was the reduction in the rate of losses.

German divisions in June 1944 were near their authorized strengths. The 134th German Division received the 1003rd March Battalion in late February 1944 to replace losses in defensive battles in January and February. At the same time, the service elements of the division were forced to sacrifice more men under the new table of organization. These men and the battalion of new replacements re-formed the 445th Infantry Regiment and restored the division to seven battalions. The 134th Division received more replacements and returning wounded, as well as new weapons, in April. As a result, the division not only filled its units to authorized strength but was overstrength, because of the wounded returning to the division. In view of the surplus of manpower, from four to six soldiers from each battalion were sent home to Germany on leave.

The division was further reinforced by the attachment of ten assault guns from the 244th Assault Gun Brigade. At the beginning of June 1944, all of the infantry battalions were at full strength, and the divisional commander was able to rotate rifle companies from the front line to rest periods in the rear.

A similar situation of plentiful replacements existed in the 260th Division in Army Group Center. The 260th was re-formed as a three-regiment, seven-battalion formation in April 1944. During June, the 260th Division was busily improving the defenses of its sector, an effort characterized as intensive. A training school was established for noncommissioned officers, an indication that many new recruits had been added during the month. On 20 June 1944, the 260/22 March Company (the twenty-second company of returning wounded sent to the 260th Division) arrived from Stuttgart with 227 men. Returning wounded were sent in companies, while new recruits came in battalions. Because all of the units of the 260th Division were overstrength, the returning wounded were distributed evenly to the seven battalions. Along with all of the other divisions in the 4th Army, the divisional antitank battalion received new 75 mm antitank guns and 20 mm antiaircraft guns. The 1st Company of the antitank battalion was sent back to Mielau in Germany in mid-June for training with new assault guns. Also in June, the 14th Company of each infantry regiment received a platoon of three 75 mm antitank guns and two platoons armed with hand-held antitank rocket launchers.

The surplus of men probably prevailed in most of the divisions in Russia in June 1944. The improvements in the 134th and 260th Divisions reflected a plentiful supply of men and weapons for the Russian front, rather than a shortage because of the diversion of men and material to France.

The panzer divisions were also upgraded in early 1944. In 1944 the panzer division had an authorized strength of one panzer regiment with 180 tanks and two panzer grenadier regiments, each with two battalions. One of the four panzer grenadier battalions was equipped with lightly armored half-tracks that could accompany tanks; the remainder rode in trucks and dismounted when fighting commenced.

The German panzer division Type 43 table of organization included a Panzer IV battalion with eighty-six tanks and a Panther battalion with seventy-three tanks. In addition there were eleven command tanks and four reconnaissance tanks. The artillery regiment included twelve Wasps (self-propelled 105 mm howitzers) and six Hummels (self-propelled 150 mm howitzers).

Panzer divisions rarely remained at full strength once a battle began. Despite a miraculous performance by German repair crews, who returned damaged tanks to action within a few days, tank battalions were often reduced to only forty tanks.

Assault-gun units in the German army were used for infantry support and to support tank units. The German panzer division had a panzer jäger battalion, with about forty assault guns. The German assault-gun brigade designed for infantry support received its nomenclature from the artillery and its contained batteries rather than from companies. In 1944 the assault-gun brigade consisted of a staff with three assault guns, three combat batteries, and an infantry battery armed with assault rifles. The gun batteries had fourteen assault guns— either Hetzers with L48 75 mm guns on a Czech T38 chassis, or Jagdpanzer IVs with long-barrel L70 75 mm guns—for a total of forty-five assault guns in the brigade.

The Germans also formed heavy tank-destroyer battalions. The Ferdinand was armed with an L71 88 mm gun (more powerful than those on the Tiger tanks); the Jagdpanther was armed with an L71 88 mm gun on a Panther chassis; and the Jagdtiger was armed with an L55 128 mm gun on a Tiger chassis. The German assault-gun brigades and tank-destroyer battalions were attached to army corps to act as tank destroyers and closely support counterattacks against Soviet armored spearheads.

In addition to improved weapons, the Germans had a bountiful supply of men to create new divisions as a result of the "million men to the front" decree. The Replacement Army had been creating new divisions at a rapid rate since 1939, as seen in previous chapters. The process of creating divisions continued at a slower pace in January and February 1944. Suddenly in February the process stopped and did not resume again until late July 1944. There is no apparent reason why new divisions could not have been formed between February and July.

In July and August 1944, after the coup failed to dispose of Hitler, the process of creating divisions resumed, with the formation of fifty-four divisions. The delay in forming new divisions had a great impact upon the German war effort, because an operational reserve was absolutely essential to counter the anticipated offensives in the East and the West in June 1944. Instead of having a reserve of twenty-eight infantry divisions available in the West and thirty-two in the East, there were practically no divisions in reserve. As will be seen in the description of the battles in France and Russia in June and July 1944, because few additional divisions were available to contain the offensives, German commanders had to rely on the slender forces available before the attacks began. The only reinforcements came from thinning out other fronts, which already were stretched thin.

In the East there were few if any troops in the second and third defense zones, a critical requirement for "elastic defense," which gave ground at a high cost to the attacker. The Russians had contained one of the most powerful offensives of the war at Kursk in 1943 with an elastic defense. Once the Germans penetrated the first line, they had been subjected to counterattacks by reserve divisions while the Russians in the first line retreated to the second line. The survivors of the first line made the second line stronger than the first had been. To break through the second line required an immense effort by the Germans. Once the Germans succeeded, the Russian survivors retreated to the third line, reinforcing the troops already there. The third line proved to be too tough for the Germans to crack, and the Kursk attack was called off.

The Germans themselves had developed the concept of elastic defense, in World War I, but the Russians used it to defeat the blitzkrieg. In White Russia in 1944 the Germans lacked the reserve divisions to occupy second and third defensive lines properly. Once the Russians broke through the first line, the second and third lines were quickly penetrated as well. The lack of troops for these lines was the direct result of the retention of battalions in the Replacement Army.

In the West there were not enough infantry divisions available to form even a first line of defense. Panzer divisions were assigned sectors, is if they were infantry, on the Normandy front in June. Meanwhile 600,000 men remained in battalions in Germany in the Replacement Army.

The creation of fifty-four new divisions in the six weeks beginning in late July shows that the resources to create the divisions were available in the months before. Creating sixty divisions in the twelve weeks from March to May 1944 would have been a far easier task. In the East the corps detachments and divisional groups could have provided cadres for thirty-two divisions, while in the West the occupation, reserve, and replacement divisions could have been transformed into infantry divisions. There was ample manpower in the Replacement Army to flesh out the divisions; over 400 combat replacement battalions had been formed and were ready to move in June 1944. The men in these battalions were available in March and April and could have been sent to new divisions rather than languishing in camps in Germany.

The following scenario, therefore, would have been possible on both fronts. In the West there were sixteen occupation divisions with six battalions, mostly overage or limited-service men and Ost troops. There were sixty Ost battalions assigned to occupation divisions in the West. Each of these occupation divisions could have been re-formed as a mobile infantry division, as was done with the four occupation divisions in the Balkans in April 1943. For example, the 714th Occupation Division was converted to the 714th Jäger Division; the older men in the division were replaced by young men from Military Districts I, II, III, and X. The two regiments (721st and 741st) were redesignated jäger regiments. The 661st Artillery Battalion was reinforced to form an artillery regiment. The engineer and signal companies became battalions. New motorcycle and antitank battalions were formed. All this was accomplished in a few weeks in 1943.

In France the sixteen former occupation divisions could have created fortress brigades of four battalions of limited-service men, who would have continued to man the Atlantic Wall with a minimum of service troops. An Ost battalion and an additional *Landesschutzen* (home guard) battalion from Germany could have increased these brigades to six battalions.

The command structure, service element, and approximately a thousand combat-fit noncoms and officers from each of the occupation divisions could have been sent to either French or German training camps and joined with seven combat replacement battalions from Germany. Divisions could have been formed with three regiments and a fusilier battalion, as was done in the Twenty-second Wave. Each division would have retained a battalion of Ost troops and converted them to service troops, as was the practice on the Eastern Front. Because the division would have continued to receive its replacements from the same battalion in Germany, there would have been no need to alter the replacement structure.

As an example of the process, the 716th Infantry Division was an occupation division in the Caen area; it consisted of the 726th and 736th Infantry Regiments (each with three battalions), the 716th Artillery Regiment, the 716th Reconnaissance Company, the 716th Engineer Battalion, and the 716th Signal Company. In April 1944 the division received the 439th and 642nd Ost Battalions as fourth battalions in each regiment. The older men could have been transferred to a new 801st Fortress Brigade—four battalions of older men, an artillery battalion, and a signal platoon. A *Landesschutzen* battalion could have been transferred from Germany.

The brigade could have retained the 439th Ost Battalion while the 642nd Ost Battalion went to the new division to provide service personnel. Experienced noncoms and combat-fit men from the old division's battalions could have been transferred to the new division. The new 716th Division could have created a third regimental headquarters, the 706th, as was actually done in November 1944.

There were dozens of replacement and training battalions in Military District VI that could have provided combat replacement battalions for the new division. The division could have received combat replacement battalions from the 328th, 195th, 75th, and 515th Replacement and Training Battalions, as was done in April 1945. The artillery regiment could have been reinforced by a battalion from the 260th Artillery Replacement Battalion, in Ludwigsburg, and another from District VI.

The new battalions could have been assembled in the Elsenborn training area, in District VI, in February 1944 and sent to join the 716th Division in France. After two months' training, the division would have been ready on 1 April 1944. Gen. Wilhelm Richter, the commander of the old 716th Division, would have commanded the new division, and a colonel of one of the regiments could have commanded the new fortress brigade.

The 716th Division had been created as part of the Fifteenth Wave in May 1941 from replacement battalions in the 166th Division staff, in Bielefeld, and the 156th Division staff, in Cologne. The division could continue to draw replacements from the 328th Replacement Battalion, in Aachen.

A similar process could have been used in the East to re-create the needed thirty-two new divisions from the corps detachments and the division groups. There were six corps detachments in Russia in the spring of 1944, with division groups from sixteen divisions. In addition, sixteen more divisions had been reduced to groups and attached to other divisions as third infantry regiments. To reconstitute the eighteen divisions that lacked a single infantry regiment would have required two combat replacement battalions and an artillery replacement battalion each, a total of thirty-six combat replacement battalions. The process would create two additional divisions, those that had been part of the corps detachments.

The thirty divisions that had been reduced to division groups would require five combat replacement battalions each plus three artillery replacement battalions, a total of 150 combat replacement battalions and ninety artillery replacement battalions. The net gain would have been thirty-two new divisions, including the two from the corps detachments. The six corps detachments would have been lost, but they could have been replaced by upgrading security and field training divisions that were used in combat in White Russia in July 1944. An additional twenty-four combat replacement battalions would have provided the manpower for the conversion.

A total of 216 infantry combat replacement battalions and ninety artillery replacement battalions would have been required to create thirty-two divisions and replace the six corps detachments, slightly more than half of the 400 infantry replacement battalions waiting to be shipped in July 1944. Surplus service personnel were available as a result of the reduction of the number of service units under the "million men to the front" program. The Ost battalions were a source of hiwis, if volunteers were not found in the prisoner of war camps.

Most of the divisions in the corps detachments were reconstituted beginning in July 1944. In light of the availability of 600,000 replacements in the spring, there is no reason that this reorganization could not have been done earlier.

We can present a hypothetical restoration process for the 262nd Infantry Division. The division was abolished in November 1943 because of heavy losses and re-formed as the 262nd Division Group, with the 462nd and 482nd Regimental Groups, in Corps Detachment D of Army Group Center. The division staff was sent to France to form the 277th Division in the Twenty-second Wave. Battalion staffs were sent to other new divisions. The 262nd Division had received its replacements from the 482nd Replacement Battalion, in Mistelbach, Austria, in Military District XVII. There were more than twenty replacement battalions in District XVII; finding five combat replacement battalions would have been no problem. In late 1944 the XVII District sent more than fifty-three replacement battalions to divisions. The five battalions plus some artillery and service personnel necessary to rebuild the 262nd Division in February 1944 could have been assembled in a training camp in East Prussia and returned to the front in two months or less. These battalions did not lack training and would have assimilated rapidly into the reconstituted division. One must remember that even the new recruits coming from the Replacement Army had more than three years of military training, including firing machine guns in the Hitler Youth before they were inducted. The returning wounded who provided the officers and noncoms for the combat replacement battalions had two or more years of combat experience.

A total of sixty divisions could have been formed in the first six months of 1944. Most of the formations listed in the chart below were re-formed in August and September after 800,000 men had been reported lost (killed or captured) to the Allies in the West and to the Russians in White Russia during the months of June and July.

The Replacement Army had more men available in early 1944 than at any other time during the war with, as we have seen, at least 600,000 trained men ready for assignment, many of them returning wounded who would return to their original division. The complete program as outlined for the production of sixty divisions would have required fewer than 400,000 combat-fit men, 100,000 limited-service men, and 120,000 hiwis. The Germans did recruit 30,000 hiwis from the camps during this period.

Most replacement battalions could produce about a thousand men per month, including newly trained recruits and returning wounded. Over the period January to April 1944, some replacement battalions turned out 4,000 men, more than enough to maintain their associated infantry divisions with replacements during a period of restricted activity and to provide 2,000 men or more for new units.

The new formations would have taken four paths, each of which had been used before or would be later. The first path was to restore the division groups on the Russian front to full divisions, which was accomplished after July, when fewer trained men were available. There were four regiments and fourteen division groups in Corps Detachments A through F, as shown in Table 5.4 Two of the corps detachments included two regiments of the respective former divisions. These

Table 5.4
Division Groups in Corps Detachments

Division Group	District	Repl Bn	City
A Det. 161	I	2	Allenstein
293	III	479	Landsberg
355	V	195	Konstanz
B Det. 112	XIII	260	Passau
255	IV	475	Dobeln
332	VIII	38	Duss
C Det. 183	XIII	302	Weiden
217	I	346	Allenstein
339	IX	459	Eisenach
D Det. 262	XVIII	I/482	Mistelback
56 (2 regiments)	IV	192	Dresden
E Det. 86	X	6	Lubeck
137	XVII	II/462	Krumau
251	IX	459	Eisenach
F Det. 123	III	338	Crossen
62 (2 regiments)	VIII	183	Glatz

two divisions would be restored by the addition of two combat replacement battalions.

There were sixteen additional division groups attached to divisions taking the place of missing regiments (see Table 5.5).

The thirty division groups could have been restored to full division status by supplementing the group headquarters, making them division headquarters. After four years of war there were many trained commanders and staff officers available in the German army; the officer shortage was in captains and lieutenants in the rifle companies. Two thousand hiwis could have staffed the service elements. Another thousand limited-service men could have filled out the service echelon.

The two existing battalions of the group could have provided cadres for the seven rifle battalions. The primary replacement and training battalion in Germany for each division could have provided two battalions. The other three battalions could have been provided by other replacement and training battalions in the division's military district. The artillery battalion in the group would have been restored

Table 5.5
Division Groups Attached to Divisions

Group	Division	District	Repl. Bn.	City
38	62	XI		
39	106	VI		
52	197	X		Kassel
113	337	XIII		
125	258	V	56	Ulm
167	376	VII	91	Kempten
216	102	XI	348	Hameln
223	168	IV	385	Bohm
268	36	VII	468	Fussen
321	110	XI	588	Hannover
323	88	V	14	Konstanz
327	340	XVII	II/132	Znaim
328	306	II	202	Gustrow
330	342	VII	316	Augsburg
333	294	III	50	Küstrin
387	302	VII	61	Munich

to regimental size with four battalions, using the existing battalion as cadre and men from the artillery replacement battalions.

The second path was upgrading an occupation division. Sixteen occupation divisions in France could have been upgraded to full mobile divisions in a similar fashion. Some occupation divisions were in fact upgraded during this period, but the Replacement Army did not make the men available to do more. Each occupation division could have formed a fortress brigade (consisting of four battalions of limited-service men), an Ost battalion of Russian volunteers, and a *Landess-chutzen* battalion. One or more battalions of captured artillery pieces could have supported the brigade, as could have the artillery installed in fortifications, with the new fortress brigades continuing to guard the coastline. The headquarters of one of the regiments of the old division could have supplied the command structure for the new fortress brigade, with a thousand limited-service men or hiwis providing service support.

The occupation divisions could have retained their headquarters and created two new regimental headquarters. The combat-fit men in the old division could have provided cadres for the five new battalions. The bulk of the men could come from a battalion of the primary replacement battalion and four more battalions from replacement units in the appropriate military district. The existing artillery battalion would provide cadre for a full regiment, with recruits from artillery replacement battalions (see Table 5.6).

Eight divisions could have been created using the reserve divisions in France. These reserve divisions were usually filled with recruits finishing their training and needed only some experienced cadre to transform them, as was done a few months later. There was a plentiful supply of experienced men among the returning wounded and the other divisions in France, so the difficulties of this procedure would not have been insurmountable (see Table 5.7).

The final four divisions could have been formed using replacement division headquarters in the military districts that contributed least to the program—I, II, XII, and XVIII. These districts included the 401st, 402nd, 412th, and 418th Division headquarters. Similar divisions had been used to form field army and reserve divisions in the past.

The sixty divisions could have been created in a series of four waves, each with fifteen divisions, in January, February, March, and April 1944, respectively (see Table 5.8).

Table 5.6
Occupation Divisions

Div.	District	Repl Bn	City
47	VI	78	Bonn
48	XI	588	Hannover
49	XI	17	Braunschweig
242	II	478	Stargard
243	XVII	I/486	Wels
244	I	311	Bischofsburg
245	V	14	Mulhouse
265	XI	12	Halberstadt
266	V	335	Mulhausen
708	VIII	350	Morchingen
709	X	490	Heide
711	XI	17	Braunschweig
712	XIII	352	Luxemburg
715	V	470	Baden-Baden
716	VI	18	Bielefeld
719	III	178	Potsdam

Table 5.7
Reserve Divisions in France

Div.	District	Repl.Bn.	City
148	VIII	461	Mahr Schonberg
157	VII	19	Munich
158	VIII	406	Rokitnitz
159	IX	106	Aschaffenburg
165	V		
166	VI/XX		
182	XVII	II/130	Vienna
189	IX	57	Siegen

Table 5.8

Division	District	Type
	First Wave	
Russia (all division groups)		
161	I	A Corps
293	III	A Corps
355	V	A Corps
112	XIII	B Corps
255	IV	B Corps
332	VIII	B Corps
38	XI	Div Group
39	VI	Div Group
France		
47	VI	Occupation
49	XI	Occupation
709	X	Occupation
711	XI	Occupation
712	XIII	Occupation
245	V	Occupation
243	XVII	Occupation
	Second Wave	
Russia		
183	XIII	C Corps
217	I	C Corps
339	IX	C Corps
137	XVII	D Corps
262	XVIII	D Corps
52	X	Div Group
113	XIII	Div Group
125	V	Div Group
France		
244	I	Occupation
242	II	Occupation
719	III	Occupation
715	V	Occupation
716	VI	Occupation
48	XI	Occupation
708	VIII	Occupation

Table 5.8   Continued

Division	District	Type
	Third Wave	
Russia		
86	X	E Corps
137	XVII	E Corps
251	IX	E Corps
62	VIII	F Corps
123	III	F Corps
167	VII	Div Group
216	XI	Div Group
223	IV	Div Group
France		
708	VIII	Occupation
265	XI	Occupation
165	V	Reserve
148	VIII	Reserve
157	VII	Reserve
158	VIII	Reserve
159	IX	Reserve
	Fourth Wave	
Russia (all Division Groups)		
268	VII	
321	XI	
323	V	
327	XVII	
328	II	
330	VII	
333	III	
387	VII	
France		
162	VI/XX	Reserve
189	IX	Reserve
182	XVII	Reserve
401	I	Replacement Division
402	II	Replacement Division
412	XII	Replacement Division
418	XVIII	Replacement Division

Germany had been at war for more than four years and had many experienced men to serve as cadres for new battalions and companies. The Hitler Youth provided years of military training before boys turned seventeen or eighteen and entered the army. In my own case, in basic training after three years in the Junior ROTC in high school, I knew more than the instructors about map reading, organization, and other topics. The Hitler Youth training was far more intense.

Forming sixty new divisions would have merely dented the number of replacements available and would have enabled the Germans to fight an effective delaying action in June, July, and August, probably avoiding the costly encirclements on both fronts. There were sufficient men to form more than fifty divisions in August and September 1944, even after the heavy German losses in June and July. One cannot ignore the basic numbers. The "million men to the front" program added a million men to the Replacement Army, enough to rebuild or create approximately 100 divisions. The forty-one divisions lost in 1943 were re-formed or replaced, leaving, again, 600,000 surplus men in the Replacement Army.

The lack of a German effort to increase the number of divisions in early 1944 deprived the fronts of a strategic reserve. The divisions available were not enough to stop the combined efforts of the Allies on the East and West, because a large number of men were held in Germany. After 20 July 1944, in about six weeks, the Germans created fifty-four new divisions—too late to delay the inevitable end of the war. Germany could not replace the 800,000 men who had been killed or made captive in June and July, but even without them the German army fought on for eight months. If they had not lost those men or replaced casualties as they occurred in the summer of 1944, the war would have continued for many more months.

6

The Catastrophe in France

June 1944 marked the beginning of the most disastrous summer of the war for Germany. The invasion of France and the attack on White Russia placed unbearable burdens on the German army. The variation of the two attacks led to different reactions; the West required a steady stream of combat replacement battalions, and the East desperately needed additional divisions to seal off Russian breakthroughs. Neither was possible, because of the restrictive actions of the Replacement Army officers involved in the conspiracy against Hitler.

In the East, Army Group Center needed trained combat divisions to fill gaps. The other army groups were reluctant to transfer divisions. In France, the German 7th Army was able to match the Allied buildup, division for division, by taking divisions from other armies in France. Infantry and panzer divisions were transferred to Normandy in a steady stream, notwithstanding the Allied attempt to block the rail lines. Even the 15th Army provided divisions. Although the fable of the success of the deception of a second landing at Calais persists today, Hitler knew through intercepts of the transatlantic telephone calls between Roosevelt and Churchill that a second landing would not take place. However, according to the ironclad rule that to reveal the data is to reveal the source, Hitler did not completely strip the 15th Army but instead reduced it to occupation divisions, which were useful only in their coastal defenses, and two mobile infantry divisions in reserve. The Germans pulled additional divisions from southern France, the Netherlands, Denmark, and Norway in the first two months.

The German problem in Normandy was the fierce daily combat, which caused considerable casualties on both sides. Whereas the Allied replacement system worked well, delivering 80,000 replacements to the American First Army in the first two months, the German Replacement Army begrudged every man until the failure of the coup removed the officers who had been constraining the sending of replacements. In the first two months the German 7th Army received only 10,000 men to replace 80,000 losses, reducing its infantry divisions to regiment-sized combat groups. The refusal to release replacement battalions in June caused the German divisions in Normandy to lose most of their combat strength by the end of June. One American officer commented at the time that the reason the Germans did not receive replacements was that their system was so complex.

The other facet of the conspirator's work in the Replacement Army, stopping the creation of new divisions, was especially noticeable in France. The abrupt change in program that occurred in February 1944, when the Replacement Army should have been creating fifteen new divisions each month, can best be illustrated by examining the flow of divisions in and out of France from June 1943 to June 1944. The details of the flow are shown in Table 6.1. The table shows the additions and subtractions from the divisions that were in France in May 1943. The additions were either newly formed divisions or burned-out divisions from Russia. The departures were combat-ready divisions sent to either Russia or Italy, in most cases.

From July to November 1943 Germans in France provided twenty-two divisions primarily to Italy while creating or rebuilding fifteen. From November 1943 to June 1944 twenty-four divisions were created or rebuilt, and only three were sent, apparently carrying out Hitler's directive to build an army to protect France from invasion. The net gain was twelve divisions for the year, but most of the gain came from February to June 1944, twelve additions versus one departure. Only three new divisions were created between February and June 1944, while nine burned-out divisions arrived in those five months. During the same five-month period the Replacement Army

Table 6.1
Flow of Divisions to and from France, June 1943 to June 1944

Month	Arrivals	Departures
June 1943	19 LW, 265, 266	328, 1 Pz, 16 Pz
July 1943	264, 334, 21 Pz	3 PG, 29 PG
August 1943	13 SS, 12 SS Pz 113, 305, 1 Para, 2 Para, 24 Pz	65, 26 Pz, 44, 76,
September 1943	25 Pz, 242, 243	94, 297
October 1943	244, 245, 3 Para	389, 14 Pz
November 1943	349, 352, 353, 17 SS PG	264, 334, 356, 371, 376, 384, 25 Pz
December 1943	70, 271, 272, 275, 276, 277	
January 1944	47, 48, 49, 77, 91, 2 Pz	715, 60 PG
February 1944	84, 85, 5 Para	13 SS
March 1944		
April 1944	331, 9 Pz, 116 Pz, 2 SS Pz	349
May 1944	Lehr P, 1 SS Pz, 2 Para	
June 1944	11 Pz, 19 Pz	
Total	40 Additions	29 Departures

refused to release trained recruits or returning wounded, troops that could have been used to create twenty-eight new divisions at the rate of seven per month. The number of divisions created in previous months had declined rapidly from six in December 1943 to five in January 1944, to three in February, and none in March. The men available in replacement battalions in Germany were sufficient not only to have continued the program of forming new divisions but to have expanded it.

The presence of an additional twenty-eight infantry divisions in France in June 1944 would have made a considerable difference and might have delayed the second front for an additional year, as Churchill persistently argued. As we shall see, the German lack of infantry divisions was an ongoing problem in June and July; it forced the Germans to employ panzer divisions in defensive tasks for which they were ill suited.

On 6 June 1944 the German army in France had fifty-four divisions plus reserve divisions consisting of training battalions. Many of the infantry divisions were occupation divisions, with older infantrymen and Soviet prisoners of war. In May 1944 the German 7th Army had twenty-three Ost battalions, one or two in each of the occupation divisions. Despite the knowledge that the invasion was eminent and that there was a huge surplus of men in the Replacement Army, little if any attempt was made to upgrade the occupation divisions by replacing the Ost battalions and substituting younger men in the rifle companies.

In January 1944, despite the directive to hold troops in France, divisions were sent to other theaters. Although the 715th Division had been fully motorized and made part of the Panzer Group reserve, it was ordered to Italy in January to help contain the Allied landing at Anzio. The 60th Panzer Grenadier Division was sent to Russia, and the 13th SS Division went to the Balkans in February.

In the East in March the Red Army attacked in the south, and Hungary threatened to make terms with the Russians. Hitler ordered the occupation of Hungary by two divisions from the Replacement Army, two divisions from the Balkans, and Panzer Lehr Division from France. Panzer Lehr returned in May, but the other four divisions went from Hungary to the Russian front.

In the first week of March the First Panzer Army was surrounded in Russia, and reinforcements were desperately needed. The 361st Division was sent from Denmark and was replaced by a newly formed division. The 349th Division was sent from France and was replaced by the recently formed 331st Division.

In the next six weeks the Russian front quieted down. In May 1944 the Panzer Lehr Division returned to France from Hungary, and the 1st SS Panzer Division came from Russia for rebuilding, along with the headquarters of the 47th Panzer Corps. The German army groups in the West in 1944 had forty-one infantry-type divisions, including occupation divisions, eleven panzer and panzer grenadier divisions, and nine reserve divisions training new recruits.

The failure to continue the process of forming new divisions after February was deliberate. Table 6.2 clearly demonstrates that there was little change in the army in the West in the crucial two months before the invasion.

Table 6.2
Additions to the Armies in the West, April and May 1944

West Command	4 April 1944	28 May 1944
Occupation Divisions	26	25
Infantry Divisions	14	16
Panzer and PG Divs.	5	10
Reserve Divisions	10	7
Total	55	58

A few reserve divisions were upgraded to combat status, which should have been the program for all of the reserve divisions. Some burned-out panzer divisions arrived from Russia, but though the Germans were well aware that the Allies would arrive in only a few months, no improvement was made in the vital two months preceding the invasion. What should have been a frantic period to reinforce the West was instead a tranquil time, marked by even less activity than usual.

Hitler's demand for reinforcements in the West was carried out on a much smaller scale than he anticipated when he ordered the addition of a million men to the army. From November 1943, when the directive was issued, to June 1944 the army in France increased by only twelve divisions, from forty-six to fifty-eight. This effort was minuscule compared to the massive mobilizations in early 1942 and in early 1943.

In the months preceding D day, when the Replacement Army should have been providing a mass of infantry divisions to contain the coming Allied invaders, its only action was to convert some reserve divisions to infantry divisions. Of the twenty-six reserve divisions formed in 1942 and 1943, half were stationed in France. Of these thirteen, only three reserve panzer divisions and three of the infantry divisions were upgraded to full combat divisions before 6 June 1944. An additional five were upgraded after the invasion, and two were disbanded.

An example of how divisions could have been formed in France in early 1944, February and March, was the creation of the 91st Air Landing Division. Preceding the landing on the beaches on 6 June, the American 82nd and 101st Airborne Divisions landed behind Utah and Omaha Beaches. They landed in the midst of the 91st German

Air Landing Division, which had been formed in January 1944 as part of the Twenty-fifth Wave in the training camp at Baumholder, in Military District XII. A few months earlier the cadre regiments had been formed from replacement battalions in Military District XII. The 1025th Reinforced Infantry Regiment and a battalion of the 1032nd Regiment provided the cadre to build two additional battalions. When complete, the division had six infantry battalions and three artillery battalions. In May 1944 the division was sent to Reims in France and reorganized as an air landing division—that is, all of its equipment could be transported by air. The artillery was replaced with mountain artillery pieces. By June 1944 the division, with the 6th Parachute Regiment of the 2nd Parachute Division attached, had been moved to Normandy by Hitler, who had learned of the proposed airdrop. Contrary to Allied accounts, the division was neither heavily armed nor specially trained to combat enemy airdrops. The 91st was described in American accounts as a tough, well trained, strong division, even though it had been assembled only five months earlier. The fighting between the 91st Division and the American paratroops was fierce, and only a remnant of the division was to remain by July.

The Allies landed on the coastal sector guarded by the 7th German Army, which included the 84th Corps in Normandy with two occupation divisions (716th and 243rd), two infantry divisions (352nd and the 709th, recently upgraded with two additional infantry battalions and two artillery battalions), and the 319th Division, occupying the Channel Islands. The 91st Air Landing Division was in reserve in the 84th Corps area. The 81st Corps included four occupation divisions (17th Luftwaffe, 346th, 245th, and 711th). The 84th Infantry Division was in reserve in the 81st Corps area. The 74th Corps, with the 266th Occupation Division and the 77th Infantry Division, held the north shore of the Contentin Peninsula, while the 25th Corps held the south shore with two occupation divisions (343rd and 265th) and two infantry divisions (353rd and 275th). The 2nd Parachute Corps was in reserve, with the 3rd and 5th Parachute Divisions. The 47th Panzer Corps, with the 2nd, 21st, 116th, and Lehr Panzer Divisions, was in reserve behind the 7th Army. The three panzer divisions (1st SS, 12th SS, and 17th SS Panzer Grenadier) of the 1st SS Panzer Corps were spread out behind the coast from Holland to the Bay of Biscay. All of these divisions were committed to the Normandy battle except for the 319th Division, in the Channel Islands.

The 15th Army included the 67th Corps, with three occupation divisions in coastal defenses and the 85th Infantry Division in reserve; the 82nd Corps, with three occupation divisions in coastal fortifications; the 89th Corps, with two occupation divisions and a reserve division in coastal defenses; and the 64th Reserve Corps, with an occupation division, a reserve division, and an infantry division, with the 19th Luftwaffe Division in reserve. The 88th Corps, with three occupation divisions, held coastal defenses in Holland.

On 6 June the Americans and British landed at five points. On the right the 4th Division of VII Corps landed on Utah Beach. The division, which met little opposition, secured the beach within two hours and soon joined up with the 101st Airborne Division. The combined force was opposed by elements of the 352nd German Infantry Division.

To the left of VII Corps, V Corps landed on Omaha Beach with the 1st and 28th Infantry Divisions and met heavy resistance. Omaha Beach was defended by the 716th Infantry Division, an occupation division with six battalions of limited-service men and two battalions of Ost troops, plus elements of the 352nd Infantry Division, described as a mobile attack division.

The 50th Division of the British XXX Corps landed on Gold Beach, meeting little resistance from elements of the 352nd Division. The British I Corps landed at June and Sword Beaches against little opposition. The British 6th Airborne Division landed behind the three British beaches in the midst of the German 711th and 716th Divisions. The British paratroopers suffered heavy casualties but created havoc in the German rear, a fact that assisted the landing parties on the beaches.

As the day progressed, the Americans encountered more elements of the German 84th Corps of the 7th Army, consisting of the 243rd, 352nd, 709th, and 716th Divisions, with the 91st Division in reserve. The British encountered the 81st Corps of the 15th Army, with the 711th, 17th Luftwaffe, 346th, and 245th Divisions. Seven of the divisions that met the Allies as they landed were not top-notch—occupation divisions (243rd, 709th, 716th, 711th, 17th Luftwaffe, 346th, and 245th) made up of older men and Ost battalions equipped with non-German weapons. The 352nd, 91st, and 84th Division were field divisions with horse-drawn transport.

The 47th Panzer Corps, with the 2nd, 21st, and 116th Panzer Divisions, was spread behind the two corps. Within a few days the 12th

SS Panzer Division, Panzer Lehr, 17th SS Panzer Grenadier Division, 11th Panzer Division, 1st and 2nd SS Panzer Divisions, and 9th Panzer Divisions were on their way to Normandy. The nine panzer divisions were at full strength, as was the SS panzer grenadier division. The 21st Panzer Division had 127 Mark IV tanks, forty assault guns, and twenty-four 88 mm guns.

The nine panzer divisions arrived within days to block the advance of the Allies. In contrast, in the East there were only two panzer divisions in reserve in the entire Army Group Center, and only two additional panzer divisions arrived in the following weeks. The lack of infantry reserves forced the German 7th Army to use panzer divisions to hold frontline sectors rather than mounting counterattacks. The lack of troops to attack persistently was a leading cause of the failure of the Germans to contain the beachheads.

Backing up the first line were the 21st Panzer Division, which attacked on 6 June; the 12th SS Panzer Division, which arrived on 7 June; the Panzer Lehr, which arrived on 9 June; and the 17th SS Panzer Grenadier Division, which arrived on 12 June. Farther back were the 116th Panzer Division, north of the Seine River; the 2nd Panzer Division at Amiens, which arrived on 13 June; the 11th Panzer Division at Bordeaux, which was en route on 9 June; the 1st SS Panzer Division in Belgium, which arrived on 10 June; the 2nd SS Panzer Division in Toulouse, which was en route on 9 June; and the 9th Panzer Division in Avignon, which remained in place to protect the south of France.

The common interpretation is that the Allied air forces sealed off the battlefield: in fact, however, the Germans were able to deliver a steady stream of units to the front, eleven divisions in six days, coming from as far as Bordeaux and Toulouse. All of these divisions traveled by train, despite the air attacks and French Underground attempts to destroy the tracks. Damage to rails is relatively easy to repair unless a locomotive is blown up on the track or a bridge is destroyed. Even then the German repair crews were able to repair the damage or find an alternate route. The trains continued to move at night.

The German army relied heavily on the railways in the rear area. For distances of less than a hundred miles, German divisions were moved in part by rail and in part by road. A German infantry division of 10,000 men had only 543 motor vehicles and 218 motorcycles, plus 726 horse-drawn vehicles. The horse-drawn and motor vehicles went by road, the troops moved by rail or marched, and the supplies were shipped by rail. This part-rail, part-road movement had many disadvantages. Above all, the troops were separated from their weapons, supplies, and ammunition, and when the division was moving into a combat zone, rarely did all three arrive simultaneously. The men arrived first, then the supplies, and finally the vehicles.

Although an infantry division with fit young men could march up to twenty miles a day for long periods, the column stretched out for twenty-five miles on a road and made an ideal target for fighter-bombers. Therefore, it could march only at night, with strict road discipline and at a slower pace. The panzer and panzer grenadier divisions moved more swiftly. They had enough vehicles to move everything with their organic (i.e., permanently assigned) equipment, at the rate of seven to ten miles per hour. The only six hours of darkness in June, however, limited the movement of troops, vehicles, and trains. A panzer division going from Paris to Caen would be halfway there by the time the last unit left Paris, but during the extremely short nights of the European summers a panzer division needed two days to reach Caen, because the fighter-bombers brought all traffic to a halt when the sun rose. Men could arrive overnight, however, if the rails were open and the unit had been loaded by nightfall. Once the combat zone had been reached, there was a terrible scramble to unload and seek cover before the daylight brought Allied fighter-bombers.

To move an infantry division any considerable distance, the Germans, having very little motor transport, had to rely on the rails. The capacity of the French railroads was enormous, if inflexible. A double-track railroad could move thirty trains in one direction per day, possibly forty-eight if all went well. Even a single track, very rare in Western Europe, could accommodate ten trains in each direction per day, despite delays at sidings to allow oncoming trains to pass. In an emergency, the single track could be reserved for one-way traffic and move thirty trains a day. Trains moved at up to sixty miles per hour, at least 500 miles a day. The Germans could move a division from any point in Europe within a few days on each rail line. Loading and unloading were the greatest obstacles.

From the south of France nearly a dozen lines led from the southern border and the Mediterranean to the north. In Russia the Germans had converted the rail lines from the wider Russian gauge to the European gauge, and the essential lines were open. Elaborate security measures prevented partisan activity from interfering seriously with rail movement.

A German infantry division with its vehicles required from fifty to seventy trains. With forty men in each car, 250 cars (or five trains) could carry 10,000 men. The British believed that a German division without vehicles needed forty trains, forty locomotives, and 2,000 cars and estimated that seven divisions could move simultaneously from Russia to France. The German field manual requirement, in fact, was sixty-six trains per division. The American standard was from thirty-five to forty trains, each of about fifty cars, to move a division.

A double-track railroad could move a train every half-hour in both directions, more than enough capacity to pass a division in less than two days. Crossing Germany by rail took less than a day. Closer to the Normandy battlefield, because they could move safely only at night, trains included fewer cars, to facilitate unloading. Even in the six hours of darkness in the middle of June, twelve trains with twenty cars each could bring in 10,000 men on one of the many lines leading to the battlefield. If one train could pass, there was no reason a dozen could not pass, unless the cars had to be ferried across a river.

A rail system on occasion could work wonders, given good planning—for example, the Russian buildups for their counteroffensive in November 1942 and for the attack on Army Group Center in June 1944. In April 1943 the Germans needed divisions desperately on the Eastern Front. The 17th and 257th Infantry Divisions were moved to Russia from France in 241 trains in four days. The larger number of trains was probably the result of reducing the number of cars per train to less than twenty rather than fifty. Shorter trains were simpler to load and could be dispatched more quickly. There were seldom enough platforms or loading equipment to load more than a few dozen cars with vehicles, guns, and horses at one time. Two to twelve hours were needed to load each train.

The Germans had the means to move divisions to the Normandy front, had they been available. On 6 June the Germans began to move additional forces to Normandy. In the British sector at Caen, the Germans added the 1st SS Panzer Corps with the 12th SS Panzer Division, Panzer Lehr, the 21st Panzer Division, and the 716th Infantry Division in a matter of days.

On 6 June the 275th Division at St. Nazaire, ordered to move to Bayeux, was delayed a few days by air attacks. A battle group of the 265th Division at Lorient began to move by road to St. Lo. In Brittany the 77th and 266th Divisions were alerted but did not begin to move. Allied aircraft reported the 12th SS Panzer Division on the road at Rouen, Panzer Lehr loading on trains at Chartres, the 2nd Panzer Division loading at Amiens, and the 17th SS Panzer Grenadier Division loading south of the Loire River. All of this activity took place on the first day of the invasion.

The German armored reinforcements arrived quickly. On the evening of 6 June elements of the 21st Panzer Division attacked the British 3rd and Canadian 3rd Divisions. The 81st Corps (346th, 711th, an element of the 716th, and a battle group of the 21st Panzer Divisions) of the 15th Army tried to destroy the 6th Airborne Division. A battle group of the 346th Division was ferried across the Seine River to assist the 711th Division in fighting the 6th British Airborne Division. In one day the Germans were able to move more reinforcements to Normandy than Army Group Center received in a month.

On 7 June the Germans began to gather forces in earnest. The 2nd Panzer Division was ordered from Amiens, the 1st SS Panzer Division from Belgium, and the 2nd SS Panzer Division from Toulouse. To form the 2nd Parachute Corps the 77th Division at St. Malo was ordered to the Contentin Peninsula, along with the 17th SS Panzer Grenadier Division south of the Loire. Also, the 3rd Parachute Division was to move from Brittany. The arrival of the reinforcements indicates that the rail lines were still usable, but there were few available infantry divisions in Germany or France. Not until late July did the Replacement Army begin to react to the crisis in France and Russia.

In France, the race to build up a sizable force and the battle of attrition both began on the second day. The contest was between the Allied LSTs (landing ship tanks) and the French railroads—which could deliver more divisions to the Normandy front? The race was neck and neck for the first month. The German divisions came from other armies in France for the most part, while the Allied divisions came from Britain. By the end of June the Germans had reached the bottom of the barrel, but the Allies continued to pour in fresh divisions. The deciding factor was the lack of the new German divisions that should have been formed in the spring. The battle of attrition also was won by the Allies, who delivered replacements at a rate of ten to one—again the result of the refusal of the Replacement Army to send forward combat replacement battalions.

On 7 June the U.S. V Corps had five regiments ashore, opposed by a regiment of the German 352nd Division, the 30th Mobile Brigade, and the remnants of the occupation divisions. The 30th Mobile Brigade arrived on bicycles on 7 June. The U.S. VII Corps landing was opposed by the 709th, 243rd, and 91st Air Landing Divisions, the 6th Parachute Regiment, and independent tank and anti-tank battalions.

The Germans began to call in more forces. On 7 June the Germans ordered the 77th Division at St. Malo to start for Normandy, along with the 3rd Parachute Division in Brittany. The 77th German Division moved from Brittany with relatively little interference from Allied air forces, which were, even at that crucial time on the second day of the landing, unable to control the roads. After dark the Germans could move freely both on the railroads and the highways. The air effort was concentrated on the bridges, which could not be easily repaired.

On 8 June the objective of VII Corps (which would be reinforced by the U.S. 9th Division on 9 June) was to cut off the northern part of the Contentin Peninsula. The U.S. 4th Infantry and 82nd Airborne Divisions attacked the German defensive line, which held until 12 June with the 709th, 243rd, and 91st Divisions, each of which had been reduced to battle groups the size of regiments. On 13 June the U.S. 90th Division was added to the attack, and on the German line, the 265th Battle Group arrived on 14 June.

In the V Corps sector on 9 June, the U.S. 29th Division along with the 2nd Division pressed back the remnants of the German 352nd Division. By the evening of 9 June the 352nd Division had only 2,500 men, fourteen artillery pieces, sixteen antiaircraft guns, and five tanks. By 10 June the German forces on the front included the 709th, 243rd, 91st, 352nd, Panzer Lehr, 12th SS Panzer, 716th, 21st Panzer, 711th, and 346th Division, plus the 6th Parachute Regiment. In transit were the 77th and elements of the 3rd Parachute, 275th, and 17 SS Panzer Grenadier Divisions.

The nearest additional Germany infantry divisions were those holding defensive positions elsewhere along the coast. Hitler's reluctance to take divisions from the 15th Army is often cited as a great victory for the Allied deception program. However, in the 15th Army, the only mobile divisions that had adequate horse-drawn transportation to participate in the battle in Normandy were the 85th, the 331st, and the 19th Luftwaffe Divisions. The 19th Luftwaffe moved to Italy on

16 June, and the 15th Army moved the 326th Occupation Division on 15 July to Normandy, followed by the 85th Division and the 331st on 6 August. The deception plan did hold two mobile divisions until 6 August, but that had little impact on the battle. The 344th Occupation division moved on 16 August. The occupation divisions could move only by rail, and most of their heavy weapons were either foreign or emplaced in the fortifications. When the occupation divisions arrived at the front, they had no horse-drawn transport for their supplies and weapons. The movement of two occupations divisions on 15 July and 16 August indicated the desperate need for infantry divisions. The Germans did have the rail transportation capacity to move in additional divisions, had they been available.

In the succeeding days, American and British divisions continued to land. On 10 June the Germans had the 709th, 243rd, and 91st Divisions plus the 6th Parachute Regiment facing the American VII Corps. In the V Corps area the U.S. 1st and 2nd Divisions broke through the German line at Caumont, opening a ten-mile gap. The U.S. 30th Division held the Panzer Lehr Division on one side, and the U.S. 29th Division pressed back the remnant of 352nd Division on the other side. The only unit available to plug the Caumont gap was the reconnaissance battalion of 17th SS Panzer Grenadier Division, which slowed the progress of the U.S. 1st Division near Caumont.

To stem the American advance, the German 84th Corps sent the 77th Division to Contentin, and the 9th Parachute Regiment was on the way to the front at Avranches. The remaining elements of the 17th SS Panzer Division were headed for the same area. The tracked vehicles came by rail and had to be unloaded south of the Loire River, because many of the bridges were down. By 15 June eight of the bridges across the Loire River had been destroyed by air attack, and the others had been damaged.

The 2nd Parachute Corps was arriving but was being sent to the Carentan/St. Lo area with the 3rd Parachute Division. The 353rd Division was also at St Lo. The 17th SS Panzer Grenadier Division was inserted southwest of Carentan along with Battle Group Heintz, from the 275th Division.

Hitler took action on 12 June, ordering the troops to fight to the last man. He also ordered the 2nd SS Panzer Corps, with the 9th and 10th SS Panzer Divisions, from Russia to France after calling off a proposed attack at Kovel in White Russia. The 2nd SS Panzer Corps would have had a major impact had it been left in White Russia. The desperate shortage of divisions in June forced Hitler to make this difficult decision.

On 16 June the Americans reached the west coast of the Contentin Peninsula, cut off the troops defending Cherbourg and caught the unfortunate 77th Division in a trap. On 14 June Rommel expected the Americans to isolate Cherbourg. He decided that the 709th and 243rd Divisions and a remnant of 91st could defend it and therefore ordered the 77th Division to move south out of the peninsula. However, the division did not move quickly enough and was decimated by the Americans on the road.

With the position in Normandy deteriorating, Hitler on 16 June moved up the 86th Corps from the 1st Army in the south of France, and infantry divisions from the 15th and 19th Armies. He expected that the arrival of the new divisions would enable Rommel to take the 17th Panzer Grenadier, Panzer Lehr, and the 2nd Panzer Division from the front to form a reserve. The two divisions from the 15th Army were replaced with divisions from Norway and Denmark. The 19th Army also received a division from Germany, along with some sailors converted to infantry. The three panzer divisions were to regroup and join four newly arrived panzer divisions to form a strategic reserve for Normandy. The new divisions were the 2nd SS Panzer from the south, the 1st SS Panzer Division from the Netherlands, and the 9th and 10th SS Panzer Divisions from Russia.

The arrival of the reinforcements was delayed by damage to the railroads. The tracked vehicles had to move by rail, because long road trips were slow and caused heavy wear on the tracks. However, the divisions arrived at about the same pace as new Allied divisions landed. The Germans at no time had enough forces to drive the Allies into the sea, while for the first weeks the Allies had inadequate forces to break the deadlock in the hedgerows of Normandy. Soon, however, the tide turned against the Germans, who lacked replacements to maintain their divisions; Allied divisions received a steady stream of men to replace casualties.

Despite shortages of all kinds and without replacements, the Germans continued to fight tenaciously. In the British sector on 10 June, elements of Panzer Lehr, the 12th SS Panzer Division, and 21st Panzer Division attacked the British Second Army at Caen but gained little ground. By 17 June the Germans had added the 2nd Panzer, 3rd Parachute, and elements of the 265th, 353rd, and 275th Divisions to their forces in Normandy. By the end of June more German divisions had arrived, but the grueling battle in the hedgerows was taking a heavy toll on the rifle companies, and few replacements were arriving from Germany. Many infantry divisions had been reduced to the status of battle groups, with two or three rifle battalions.

The occupation divisions of the 15th Army guarding the Channel coast were the best available. On 13 June Gen. Alfred Jodl, chief of operations, suggested to Hitler that all efforts be made to defeat the Allies in Normandy and to ignore any threat of other landings, thus freeing the divisions of the 15th Army for use in Normandy. Hitler refused to accept Jodl's plan.

The eleven occupation divisions and two infantry divisions of the 15th Army remained in the coastal fortifications north of the Seine River. The occupation divisions had neither heavy weapons nor field artillery. Their men, either elderly Germans or Soviet prisoners, surrendered when they encountered the Allies. The two reserve divisions consisted of battalions training new recruits.

The two infantry divisions, the 84th and 85th, had been formed in February 1944 near Dieppe as divisions in the Twenty-fifth Wave. The 84th Division was created from the 1022nd Grenadier Regiment and the I Battalion of the 1032nd Grenadier Regiment. The 1022nd Regiment had been formed in November 1943 in Military District VI from Replacement Army battalions, and the 1032nd Regiment had been assembled on 30 December 1943 from replacement battalions in Military District X. The division had six infantry battalions and two battalions of light field guns, along with a battalion of 88 mm guns—below the standard of a regular German division but adequate for combat.

The 85th Infantry Division was formed in February 1944 from the reinforced 1024th Infantry Regiment, which had come from the replacement battalions in Military District XII. The division, which had six infantry battalions and two artillery battalions, was considered ready for assignment in May 1944. This organization schedule could have been implemented for many more divisions, as suggested above.

The two Luftwaffe divisions had transport but were not fully equipped, and their leaders had little experience in ground warfare. The 18th Luftwaffe Division had been formed in late 1942 in France from the 52nd Luftwaffe Air Regiment. It had six infantry battalions and three artillery battalions. The division had guarded the coast near Dunkirk since 1943. In November 1943 it was reorganized as an occupation division, with seven infantry battalions and two artillery battalions, assigned at Dunkirk to the 15th Army. The 17th

Luftwaffe Division had a similar history, filling an occupation role at Le Havre.

Even had the Germans ignored the possibility of a second landing, the divisions of the 15th Army would have had serious difficulty in transforming themselves into mobile infantry divisions within a few days. Machine guns and artillery emplaced in fortifications necessarily would have been left behind and new weapons issued. Horse-drawn transport confiscated from the French would have needed service personnel to care for the horses. Those two problems, weapons and transport, could have been solved with relative ease in March and April, but under the stress of operations there was no time to accomplish the transformation. Although security divisions organized much like the occupation divisions were committed to the front in White Russia in June, their lack of artillery and heavy weapons limited their combat value. A few occupation divisions were moved to Normandy to hold quiet sectors and relieve the panzer divisions of that unprofitable task.

The absence of a program to create new divisions in the spring of 1944 was possible because Hitler was no longer able to control the minutiae as in the past. Because of his poor health, he no longer daily discussed with his generals, as in 1943, the details of each division on the front. After Hitler met with Field Marshal von Rundstedt, commanding in the West, in a bunker near Soissons on 16 June 1944, it was remarked that Hitler looked sick and tired. His hands were always busy playing with pencils and his eyeglasses, typical of people with Parkinson's disease. Rather than standing at the map table as before, he sat on a stool. The charisma was gone. He shouted at the generals, blaming them for failing to eradicate the beachhead. Rather than his usual practice of pouring out detailed instructions, he merely ordered all units to hold their positions everywhere. Unlike in past situations, he did not give specific orders to implement his policy.

In contrast, the generals preferred to trade land for casualties and withdraw to shorten the front. The commanders also wanted to transfer more divisions from elsewhere in France. Hitler insisted that the divisions in southern France remain there to defend it.

The generals managed to appear to maintain the rigid defense that Hitler ordered but to transfer a few infantry divisions and pull some panzer divisions from the line. The panzer divisions were then able to mount counterattacks. On 17 June Panzer Lehr and the 2nd Panzer Division attacked the British 30th Corps, with little success.

A few more fresh German divisions arrived and were committed piecemeal against the Americans. Three divisions reinforced the 7th Army, the newly formed 59th Infantry Division from Germany (on 22 June), the 89th Infantry Division from Norway, and the 363rd Division from Denmark (on 31 July). For the remainder of June the U.S. V Corps front was bogged down in the hedgerows as the Germans contested every meter of ground.

On 20 June the German high command ordered Rundstedt to gather six panzer divisions to attack at the boundary between the Americans and the British. Two of the panzer divisions were still in line and had to be replaced by the 276th and 277th Divisions, coming from southern France. The 1st and 2nd SS Panzer Divisions were delayed as well. On 25 June the British attacked Panzer Lehr and the 12th SS Panzer Division, forcing the Germans to throw in the lead elements of the 1st SS Panzer Division. On 26 June elements of the 2nd SS Panzer, 2nd Panzer, and 21st Panzer Divisions were added to the British sector. Individual battalions were thrown in as soon as they arrived. Finally on 29 June, the 2nd SS Panzer Corps launched an attack on the British but achieved very little.

By 2 July the Germans had added to their strength in Normandy. In southern France the 19th Army had the 4th Luftwaffe Corps, Corps Kniess, and the 62nd Reserve Corps. In the southwest the 1st Army held the Bay of Biscay shore with the 80th Corps and the 64th Reserve Corps. In Holland the 88th Corps held the coastline. At the Pas de Calais, the 15th Army held the coast with the 82nd Corps, the 67th Corps, and the 81st Corps. On the Channel coast the 7th Army had the 25th Corps and the 74th Corps in Brittany. In Normandy the 84th Corps and the 2nd Parachute Corps faced the Americans; Panzer Group West, with the 86th Corps, the 1st SS Panzer Corps, the 2nd SS Panzer Corps, and the 47th Panzer Corps, faced the British.

Reinforcements were reaching the front despite the work of Allied planes. By 2 July four divisions arrived in Normandy from Brittany, and a fifth arrived a few days later. One of the divisions came from Holland, and six came from Army Group G in the south of France. The 15th Army sent two divisions, which were replaced by divisions from Norway and Denmark.

The Germans, however, were handicapped by the lack of replacements for combat losses. Although their replacement system was more complicated than the American method of arbitrary assignment of men, the practice of returning wounded to their previous divisions had advantages. My cousin, who was wounded three times while serving with the U.S. 88th Infantry Division in Italy, went absent without leave from the hospital before he was fully recovered and made his way back to his company; otherwise he would have been sent to the replacement pool and to another division. Once back with his company, the officers managed to obtain approval of his return. The German army recognized the importance of unit association. New recruits, as noted, went to divisions composed of men from their district, which made assimilation far easier. However, the supposedly complicated system was not the reason for the lack of replacements in Normandy; the problem was that the Replacement Army refused to release any replacement battalions.

The German forces in Normandy not only lacked replacements but were also short of munitions—due more likely to refusal of the officials in Germany to send them rather than to lack of transportation. Transportation was difficult, as air attacks damaged the railroads and bridges. All of the bridges across the Seine were destroyed or damaged except those in Paris; once across the Seine in Paris, however, there was little to stop the trains from moving to Normandy. The Germans engineers worked persistently to repair damaged bridges. In one instance the German goal was to get five trains a day across one bridge (each train with at least 1,000 tons), but in one week only four trains succeeded. The bridge was repaired, however, and once in service at least a dozen trains with more than 12,000 tons of supplies could have crossed that single bridge each night. If the rail service had been as bad as pictured in the official American accounts, the people of Paris would have starved to death. My friends in Paris in 1949 complained of the quality of the food during the war but not of the quantity.

The Germans also used barges on the Seine to carry supplies to near the Normandy bridgehead. The cargoes were then moved forward eighty miles by truck and horse-drawn wagons to the army depots. Units had to move at night. Road supply was uncertain, though the 7th Army had enough trucks to carry 1,300 tons per day. The French drivers were unreliable, and the trucks were in bad repair.

There was a general shortage of supplies, especially a chronic shortage of artillery ammunition. The German 7th Army needed 3,250 tons of supplies per day (1,000 tons of ammunition, 1,000 tons of fuel, and 250 tons of rations) but was receiving only about 1,000 tons per day, the capacity of a single twenty-car train. By 1 July there was a supply deficit, and the Germans were forced to draw on stocks in the army depots.

Other factors must have been at work, because given the dense network of rails in northern France, the inability of a half-dozen trains per night to reach Normandy from Paris is unaccountable. Trains could move freely during the six hours of darkness, which was enough time for twelve trains per night on each line in passable condition. French locomotives and cars were available.

The American claim has been that repair crews could not keep up with the air and sabotage damage to the rails, even though only a few hours were needed to repair a direct hit on track. If a train had been blown up or bombed, repairing fifty feet of track was a longer process but usually took less than a day. The Russian partisans, who were far more active than the French resistance, delayed rail movement on a track in White Russia only a few days at the most. French railway employees may have contributed to the delays, but if detected, punishment was severe and instantaneous. The far-reaching difference between railroad performance in France and White Russia may have been that Germans operated and maintained the railroads in White Russia, while the French continued to operate and maintain those in France.

As a result of shortages of replacements and supplies, the Germans were in a weakened condition when the U.S. VIII Corps launched its attack on 3 July. The attack struck the 243rd, 353rd, 77th, and 17th SS Panzer Grenadier Divisions at the west end of the line. The Germans 84th Corps also had Battle Group Koenig, with elements of the 91st, 265th, and 243rd Divisions and the 2nd SS Panzer Division, in reserve. Nonetheless, although the German divisions were short of men and supplies, their situation was improving in the first week of July.

On 3 July the U.S. VII Corps attacked elements of the German 7th Army, including the 6th Parachute Regiment, a regiment of the 17th SS Panzer Grenadier Division, and elements of the 2nd SS Panzer Division. Opposing the U.S. 4th and 30th Divisions were a regiment of the 17th SS Panzer Grenadier Division and Battle Group Heinz (with three battalions from the 275th Division, elements of the 266th Division), and Battle Group Kentner, with elements of the 352nd Division.

Four days later the U.S. XIX Corps attacked with little success, running into a regiment of the 2nd SS Panzer Division. On 9 July XIX Corps continued to attack the Vire River line but stalled when the

Germans sent in Panzer Lehr to stop the drive. In July the U.S. 2nd Infantry Division tried to take St. Lo but was held back by the German 2nd Parachute Corps, with the 352nd Division, a battle group of the 353rd Division, a battle group of the 266th Division, and the 3rd Parachute Division. On 8 July the British 1st and 8th Corps again tried to take Caen, held by the 1st SS Panzer Corps, with the 21st Panzer and 12th SS Panzer Divisions, and on 9 July broke into Caen.

The fighting dragged on in Normandy without significant change for the next week. By 17 July, however, the 2nd Parachute Corps was in trouble and asking for the 5th Parachute Division from Brittany. The division arrived several days later to replace Panzer Lehr in the line. The 275th division also arrived to strengthen the 7th Army. The Americans finally took St. Lo on 18 July. The German 352nd Division tried but failed to retake the city.

The heavy fighting had produced enormous casualties on both sides. American replacements arrived in a steady stream and sustained the American divisions at near full strength. Not so on the German side, as the Replacement Army refused to release combat replacement battalions. German casualties from 6 June to 11 July were 2,000 officers and 85,000 men, but only 5,210 replacements had arrived—roughly five trainloads in five weeks, one train a week—and only 7,500 more men were promised! By 17 July casualties increased to more than 100,000, including 2,360 officers.

If the German infantry divisions had become mere shadows, the German SS panzer divisions remained powerful, receiving their replacements from the SS organization rather than the Replacement Army. On 18 July the British launched "Goodwood," an attack by three British armored divisions attempting to outflank the German position at Caen. The British encountered the 81st Corps (with the 21st Panzer Division and the 346th Infantry Division) and the 1st SS Panzer Corps (the 12th SS Panzer, 1st SS Panzer, and 272nd Divisions). To the left of these corps was the 2nd SS Panzer Corps (the 9th and 10th SS Panzer Divisions). At the start of the attack on 18 July, the British had 270 tanks. On 19 July, 131 were still operational and on 20 July only sixty-eight; the British had lost two hundred tanks in three days. Their expected breakthrough did not occur.

The breakthrough came in the American sector.

The Americans planned to break through the German line on 20 July 1944 (code-named "Cobra"), but the operation was delayed. By 25 July all of the U.S. divisions, despite heavy losses, had been restored to full strength by replacements. The American VII and VIII Corps, with 90,000 men, would attack the west end of the German line, held by the 84th and 2nd Parachute Corps, with 17,000 men.

The Germans had received some reinforcements by 22 July, including four additional infantry divisions to replace the panzer divisions on the front line in the British sector. The 277th Division replaced the 9th SS Panzer Division on 10 July; the 272nd Division replaced the 1st and 12th SS Panzer Divisions on 13 July; the 271st Division replaced the 10th SS Panzer Division on 17 July; and the 326th Division replaced the 2nd Panzer Division on 22 July. The 7th Army was ordered to relieve from frontline duty the 2nd SS Panzer Division and Panzer Lehr when the 363rd Division arrived from the 15th Army.

On 25 July the German forces facing Cobra from the coast to the east were the remnant of the 243rd Division, the remnant of the 91st Division, the remnant of the 77th Division, a battle group from the 265th Division, the 2nd SS Panzer Division, the 6th Parachute Regiment, the 17th SS Panzer Grenadier Division, the 5th Parachute Division, and Panzer Lehr. The 353rd Division was the 84th Corps reserve, and the 275th Division was the 7th Army reserve. The German divisions were worn down by combat and the lack of replacements. Panzer Lehr had only 3,200 combat-fit men on 25 July. In contrast, and as noted, the American divisions, which had suffered a higher percentage of losses, were kept at full strength by a stream of replacements.

If the German Replacement Army had released fifty or more combat replacement battalions (800 to 1,000 men each) between 7 June and 25 July at a rate of one per day, each carried by a single train, the battered divisions could have been restored to nearly full strength. A combat replacement battalion could be loaded on a single twenty-car train in Germany and reach Paris by dark. From Paris the train could travel by night, to avoid air attack, to within thirty miles of the front. The battalion could march the final distance in one or two nights. There were multiple lines from Paris to the Normandy area, one of which would have been open on most nights. Instead, the Replacement Army released only 10,000 men during the seven weeks. The 243rd, 91st, and 77th Divisions and the battle group of the 265th could have been brought up to a reasonable strength with five replacement battalions each. The effective combat strength of the forces facing VII and VIII Corps would have more than doubled. As it was, When the Americans broke the crust of the German line, they were able to race through France in the next two months. Only after the Germans had created or rebuilt nearly sixty divisions and placed them in the line would the rapid American advance come to halt.

The manipulation of troops by the Replacement Army was evident in June and led to the disasters of late July and August. There should have been twenty-eight additional German divisions in France on 6 June 1944. After the invasion the deliberate withholding of replacements was most acutely damaging in the first six weeks after D day. While the Allies provided 79,000 replacements for 61,732 losses by 30 June, keeping their divisions up to strength, only 10,000 replacements for 110,000 losses were provided by mid-July to the divisions in Rommel's army group. While American and British divisions continued to appear as such in orders of battle, the German infantry divisions appear as combat groups, usually of regimental size. Infantry divisions on both sides each lost two or three thousand riflemen in the first six weeks. The Allies replaced their losses with newly trained riflemen, while the Germans, denied the thousands of replacements in training battalions in Germany, used service troops to fill some of the ranks of the rifle companies and reduced their divisions to regiments.

The Allies had to transport their replacements across the English Channel, an all-day trip just to the beachhead; the Germans, in contrast, as we have seen, could put a battalion of replacements on a train in Germany in the morning to arrive within a few miles of the front the following morning. Despite Allied attempts to halt rail traffic, a railroad is a narrow target, and only a few hours are needed to replace fifty feet of track. For instance, despite German efforts to destroy miles of rail in northern France as they retreated, the Allies had trains running within a week or so in the territory they occupied. Therefore, moving the replacements to the front was not a major obstacle. The issue was having the Replacement Army release them in the first place.

The accepted interpretation of the inability of the Americans to continue their advance in September 1944 was that they had run out of supplies. Blame has been placed on the U.S. supply service for failure to deliver enough material, and on the Allied decision to give Field Marshal Bernard Law Montgomery a greater share of the available supplies.

In fact, however, the Allied supply service did not fail. The established supply requirement in the U.S. army was 541 tons per each division and its supporting units during normal combat, 426 tons when regrouping, and 462 tons when engaged in rapid pursuit of the enemy. Rations remained static, because the need for food did not change; equipment replacement and service supply were also assumed to remain the same in all three situations. Gasoline consumption, however, increased to 40 percent of the total during pursuit, and ammunition consumption dropped sharply during regrouping and pursuit. These supply requirements were met in France. The 450 to 550 tons per division was ample, even with somewhat lavish expenditures in certain kinds of supplies. For example, the U.S. Ninth Army expended 50 percent more tonnage for rations than the other American armies, reflecting a diversion of large stocks of food to the civilian population. Seventh Army used 70 percent more ammunition, because it was supplying the French First Army with ammunition and artillery support. The total figure of 550 tons per division was adequate for these extras.

In September 1944 Gen. Omar Bradley demanded 650 tons per division and when he received only 550 tons complained that the supply services had failed. For that reason, divisions were held back from the front and not permitted to advance to take part in the battle at the crucial point; also, attempts were made to limit gasoline supplies to Third Army. Far from failing, the supply service had exceeded demands. In September 1944, 560 tons were delivered per division, including 185 tons of clothing, vehicles, service unit material, and 144 tons of gasoline and oil, as against the normal demand in pursuit of only 462 tons. In both East and West it was the arrival of fresh German divisions that stopped the advance, not the lack of supplies.

Had the German Replacement Army created an additional sixty divisions in the spring of 1944, these divisions would have been able to contain the Allied bridgehead for a lengthy period. Such a delay had been expected by Allied planners, even with the reduced number of German divisions. With an additional twenty-eight divisions, Rundstedt could have halted the Allies short of Paris and lengthened the war by at least a year.

The North Sector

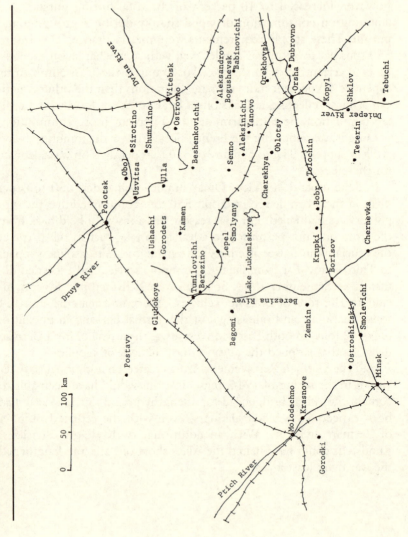

7

The Catastrophe
in the East

Simultaneous assaults in Normandy and on Army Group Center caused more losses to the Germans in June and July 1944 than in any other two months during the war. The Russian success was not the product of sending waves of riflemen against German machine guns but of the improved techniques of the Red Army and enormous concentrations of tanks and artillery in selected sectors. The torrent of explosives followed by masses of tanks broke through the German defense zones in one or two days. The only reasonable solution was defense in depth. Once a first defense zone had been compromised, the Germans should have withdrawn to a second zone, which would have required the Russians to move their artillery forward and repeat the bombardment.

Whereas in the past the Germans had had divisions in reserve in the second defense zone to provide safe haven for the troops withdrawing from the first zone, in June 1944 most of the available divisions were in the front lines. The Germans had failed to produce the necessary new divisions in the spring of 1944, either in the West nor in Germany. The impact of the lack of an occupied second defense zone was worsened by Hitler's insistence on holding ground as long as possible. The combination of holding positions too long and the lack of fallback positions made possible repeated breakthroughs by the Red Army. The blitzkrieg that followed, in which Russian armored columns plunged into the German rear, reversed the previous ratio of casualties. The Germans lost many more prisoners than ever before, and the Soviet losses of killed and wounded were far less than usual.

Fresh divisions were essential to occupy the second defense zone, which would have halted the Soviet penetrations and prevented the encirclement of German units. The lack of a fresh divisions in the East in June 1944 made slowing the Soviet offensive in White Russia impossible until the second week of July 1944, when Field Marshal Walther Model, commander of Army Group North Ukraine, finally began moving divisions from Army Group North Ukraine.

The *Valkure* units available in the Replacement Army were not sent to the front, as we have seen, because the generals plotting to kill Hitler in July 1944 planned to use units of the Replacement Army to subdue the SS and cope with civil unrest in Germany following the assassination. Rather than assembling divisions and regimental groups to cope with the emergency as in the past, the trained men were held in the replacement battalions throughout Germany. Only after the plot failed was a flood of new divisions formed. The flow of units to the fronts resumed in August, enabling the Germans to stabilize the situation on both fronts in September 1944, although the Red Army continued to advance slowly, paying the price of enormous numbers of casualties.

The massive attack in White Russia began on 22 June 1944 with a greater force than the Allies employed in all of France. The Red Army launched five major successful attacks on the Army Group Center—at Vitebsk, Bogushevsk, Orsha, Mogilev, and along the Pripyat Marsh. Because of the immense numbers of units involved, each of these attacks will be described in turn.

At Vitebsk, the 2nd Baltic Front, the northernmost Soviet front involved in the campaign, applied constant pressure on the German 16th Army to prevent its divisions from shifting south to counter the other Soviet attacking fronts, and to secure the northern flank of the breakthrough being forced on its left by the 1st Baltic Front. When after 4 July the 2nd Baltic Front attacked the German 16th Army, the Germans had necessarily weakened it to provide reserves for Army Group Center.

The 1st Baltic Front conducted the operations against Vitebsk. The German forces defending the line were the 1st Corps of the 16th Army of Army Group North, including the 205th, 24th, and 290th Infantry Divisions. In support was the 909th Assault Gun Brigade, with forty-five assault guns. Elements of the 281st Security Division were in reserve at Polotsk. The severe shortage of divisions became evident when the Germans were forced to employ security divisions, with elderly men and few heavy weapons, as reserves for the front line.

The three German divisions of the 1st Corps had been in the Polotsk area for months and were well established in their defensive areas. The 1st Corps was more than adequate to defend its sector against the Soviet 4th Shock Army and was able to release some of its divisions to assist the 9th Corps to the south as well as to protect the flank of Army Group North.

When the offensive opened on 22 June, the Russians applied pressure on the 205th and 24th Infantry Divisions, screening the rail junction of Polotsk, and continued these attacks through 25 June. On 22 June Army Group North was ordered to commit the 24th Infantry Division at Obol with an assault gun brigade to assist the 252nd German Division of the 9th Corps. As the Red Army advanced on 23 June, Army Group North ordered the 290th Division to Obol and the 212th Division to Polotsk to protect the army group's flank.

The situation remained stable until 27 June, when the Soviets advanced toward Polotsk, forcing the Germans to move the 81st and 290th Infantry Divisions to defend the city. A wide gap opened between the 16th Army to the north and the 9th Corps of the 3rd Panzer Army to the south. On 29 June, Model, the new army group commander, desperately searching for fresh divisions to plug the holes in the line to the south, requested that Army Group North be allowed to free up two divisions for use elsewhere by shortening its line and withdrawing to Polotsk. Hitler approved the retreat but demanded that Polotsk be held.

The Germans continued to feed divisions into the battle south of Polotsk to close the breach between Army Group North and the 3rd Panzer Army, desperately attempting to restore a solid front. By 30 June, however, matters were out of hand for German Army Group Center. The Russians bypassed Polotsk and advanced thirty kilometers by the evening of 30 June, pushing back remnants of the German 9th Corps and opening a large hole between the 3rd Panzer Army and the 16th Army.

On the same day the Soviets cleared Vitebsk and drove back the 9th Corps, which was unable to offer serious resistance. The 9th Corps, in full retreat, had no reserve divisions to establish a fallback position. To alleviate the situation the 16th Army extended its line south, moving the 205th and 24th Infantry Divisions and the 201st and 221st Security Divisions to reinforce the 290th and 81st Divisions of the 9th Corps. Security divisions were placed in the front for the lack of any other, even though they were woefully underequipped to fight the heavily armed Soviet divisions and soon evaporated under attack. The 212th Infantry Division was sent to Lepel, south of the gap, to help the remnants of the 252nd and 95th Divisions. Despite these measures the Soviets crossed the Ulla River and drove west, cutting the rail line between Polotsk and Molodechno.

The breach widened between the 16th Army units to the north and the scattered units of the 3rd Panzer Army. Turning north against the 16th Army on 1 July, the Soviets attacked Polotsk from three sides and broke into the city on the following day. Indicative of his inability to grasp the situation, Hitler insisted that the 16th Army launch an attack from the Polotsk area, even though it had been unable to hold the city. Rather than make the futile attack, Model urged that the divisions from the 16th Army be used to the southwest, at Molodechno, to blunt the Soviet attack. The German 16th Army was never able to react freely to the offensive and was barely able to restore contact with 9th Corps units at Molodechno. The Soviet 2nd Baltic Front effectively prevented the German 16th Army from intervening meaningfully in the battle. Army Group North was forced to look to its own problems and spared little for its southern neighbor.

The major attack on Vitebsk came from north of the city. The primary mission of the 3rd Panzer Army (the northernmost of Army Group Center's armies) was to defend Vitebsk and to prevent the Red Army from using the main road, which passed through the city toward Minsk. The key to the entire White Russian offensive was opening the road from Vitebsk to Minsk to facilitate the rapid movement of motorized units and supplies. The 1st Baltic Front was assigned the task of breaking through north of Vitebsk and driving the 9th Corps of the 3rd Panzer Army west, opening the road to Molodechno.

North of Vitebsk the 9th Corps had the 252nd Infantry Division and Corps Detachment D, created in November 1943 from the remnants of the 56th and 262nd Infantry Divisions, which had suffered heavy casualties that August. (Corps Detachment D could have been restored to two full divisions with the addition of combat replacement battalions and artillery replacements.) The 9th Corps was supported by the 245th Assault Gun Brigade, which had been formed in April 1943 to replace the 245th Battalion, lost at Stalingrad.

The Russian attack north of Vitebsk on 22 June completely surprised OKH, although the frontline troops had anticipated some activity. After a very heavy artillery barrage and air attacks, elements of seven Soviet divisions, four tank brigades, three tank regiments, and four assault-gun regiments (a total of nearly 400 armored vehicles) attacked the 252nd Division and Corps Detachment D on a twenty-kilometer front. The Soviet armies quickly broke through the German first defense zone. Without reserve divisions, the Germans were forced to detach regiments from other divisions in the line to try to seal off the penetrations—the 24th Division from the north and the 280th Regiment from the 95th Division in the south. However, these reinforcements were far from enough to stop the Russians.

At Vitebsk the Germans had constructed elaborate defenses, held by four divisions in a relatively small sector. The Russians did not repeat their past efforts to take Vitebsk by frontal assault. However, previous attacks had whittled away at the German defenses, leaving Vitebsk in a salient surrounded on three sides by the Red Army. The German garrison of Vitebsk, under the command of Gen. A. Gollwitzer of the 53rd Corps of the 3rd Panzer Army, included the 206th and 246th Infantry Divisions and the 4th and 6th Luftwaffe Field Divisions. The 201st Security Division was the only 3rd Panzer Army reserve. Obviously, if a security division was to serve as a reserve, it should have been built up to a full combat division status with the addition of combat replacement battalions.

Sensing the coming crisis, Field Marshal Ernst Busch, commanding Army Group Center, proposed withdrawing from the Vitebsk salient to shorten the line and create reserves, but Hitler would not agree; he believed that aside from the main road through Vitebsk, the poor road network in White Russia precluded any large-scale armored operations. Without control of the hard-surfaced road through Vitebsk, Hitler was convinced, the Russians could not sustain an offensive in White Russia. In the previous months, the Germans had successfully defended the Vitebsk area by concentrating their defenses on the main highway and since then had improved their defenses.

The perimeter around Vitebsk was comparatively quiet on 22 June. The second day of the offensive, 23 June, brought the Red Army success. On the 252nd Division front, the Russians drove the Germans from their defenses and separated the division from the 16th Army to the north. The beaten 252nd and 56th Divisions retreated, leaving their heavy weapons. To ease the pressure, the 24th Division and the 909th Assault Gun Brigade counterattacked, but they made little progress. By the evening of 23 June, the Russians had advanced eighteen kilometers on a sector twenty kilometers wide and were only two kilometers from the River Dvina. The 3rd Panzer Army had committed all of its reserves, and there were no reserves at the army group level, other than training and security units.

North of Vitebsk the Russians continued to attack elements of Corp Detachment D, which were scattered in the string of lakes in front of the German second defense zone, the "Tiger" line. Remnants of Corps Detachment D were pushed south toward the Dvina River immediately west of Vitebsk on 23 June. The 246th Division of the city garrison tried to create a defense line on the south bank of the river but was separated by three kilometers from Detachment D. Despite German counterattacks, the Russians broke through the second defense zone and, by evening, had crossed the West Dvina River south of Shumilino. By nightfall, Soviet antitank guns were firing on the road west from Vitebsk to Beshenkovichi. The trap was about to close.

South of Vitebsk, the Soviets cut the Vitebsk-Orsha rail line and drove on toward Ostrovno. Vitebsk was in serious trouble. The garrison commander was acutely aware of the Russian spearheads closing from the north and southwest of the city. The Soviet units surrounding Vitebsk on the east waited patiently. Gen. Georg-Hans Reinhardt, the 3rd Panzer Army commander, wanted to evacuate Vitebsk immediately, but Hitler stubbornly refused, still believing the highway was the key to the situation. However, at 6:30 P.M. Hitler approved the withdrawal of the four German divisions to the second zone of defense in the city, reducing the perimeter by at least half. By 7:30 P.M. Hitler approved withdrawal to the third defense zone, crowding the four divisions into a thirty-kilometer perimeter.

In the late afternoon of 23 June the Russians were rapidly closing the noose. Gen. R. Wuthmann, commander of the 9th Corps, abandoned any attempt to maintain contact with the garrison in Vitebsk and ordered his remaining troops to prepare to abandon the Tiger line and withdraw a further fifteen kilometers back to the third defense zone on 24 June. The third defense zone was on a line of marshes north of Obol through a series of lakes to the Dvina River and on to

Beshenkovichie. However, during the night of 23–24 June, Corps Detachment D collapsed, and the Soviets penetrated the lakes in front of the Tiger line.

Wuthmann ordered the immediate retreat to the third defense zone in front of Beshenkovichi on the Dvina River. The 252nd German Division held the west bank of the Dvina ten kilometers northwest of Beshenkovichi, but a void was opening between the division and Detachment D to the south. Another eighteen-kilometer hole opened between Detachment D, which had held Ostrovno, and the 246th Division of the 53rd Corps defending Vitebsk. By the evening of 24 June, the 9th Corps was scattered between Obol and Vitebsk.

With a reduced perimeter around Vitebsk, Gollwitzer pulled the 4th and 6th Luftwaffe Divisions from the line early in the afternoon of 24 June and sent them west to hold the road from Vitebsk to Ostrovno, but he was not permitted to use his entire corps to break out. Hitler feared that if the divisions tried to break out, all of their heavy weapons and equipment would be lost and that they would be unable to defend themselves.

Finally at 7 P.M. on 24 June, Hitler granted authority to use three of the four divisions to hold the Ostrovno road but demanded that the 206th Division continue to hold Vitebsk. The withdrawal of the 53rd Corps to a smaller perimeter allowed the Soviets to concentrate in a narrow sector southwest of Vitebsk and press north against the 206th Division, holding the city. At 11 P.M. the Russians cut the road on both sides of Ostrovno, trapping the German 4th Luftwaffe Division and the remnant of the 197th Infantry Division in Ostrovno. The remainder of the 53rd Corps, 35,000 men, was trapped in Vitebsk. A wide gash was torn in the German line from Detachment D west of Ostrovno to remnants of the 6th Corps retreating in the south.

At noon on the 24th Field Marshal Busch had requested reinforcements of at least two divisions to help restore a cohesive front. However, no divisions were available in Germany. Hitler proposed to send the 212th and 290th Divisions from the 16th Army at Polotsk and replace them with the 81st Division. The 201st and 221st Security Divisions were sent to the West Dvina River line. Army Group North Ukraine was ordered to send the 5th Panzer Division. All that could be dredged up were two infantry divisions that were already engaged in heavy fighting, two security divisions with limited amounts of heavy weapons and artillery, and a single panzer division. Even so, the army group commanders that were ordered to release these slender reserves did so reluctantly, and many days would pass before they arrived. No units were dispatched from Germany. Hitler did not explain how a few battered divisions could stop two Soviet armies. Ten fresh divisions would have made a considerable impact in the first three days; they would have prevented the destruction of the 9th and 53rd Corps.

On 25 June the Germans tried to hold the Tiger line along the Dvina River, but by noon the Soviets had crossed the river on rafts and boats. The only units available to the 3rd Panzer Army were the 201st Security Division, the 66th Security Regiment, and the Pershe Cossack Battalion, by no means enough to hold back the Soviets. The 9th Corps was under constant pressure. Beshenkovichi, held by elements of the German Detachment D, was surrounded by the Soviets advancing toward the Dvina. With the 9th Corps split into scattered units, the 24th and 290th Divisions were returned to 16th Army command to hold the flank of Army Group North.

At 1:30 P.M. on 25 June, the 3rd Panzer Army commander asked permission to abandon the Tiger line on the Dvina River and move the remnants of the 9th Corps back to a line running through Uzvitsa (about thirty-five kilometers southeast of Polotsk) to the Ulla River, to allow the troops time to establish a defense line before the Russians arrived. The 201st Security Division frantically prepared positions on the defense line. Hitler refused to allow the 9th Corps to abandon the Tiger line and withdraw to the new positions; instead, the Red Army drove the Germans out. Corps Detachment D and an assault-gun brigade were fortunate to fight their way out of Beshenkovichi. The remainder of 3rd Panzer Army tried to hold the Dvina and Ulla River lines for one more day.

At Vitebsk the 53rd Corps tried to break out on 25 June. Five divisions were encircled around Vitebsk, the 4th Luftwaffe Division was surrounded in Ostrovno, and the rest of the corps was either in Vitebsk or scattered along the road leading west. The 206th Division was still under orders to hold the city. By 2 P.M. the 4th Luftwaffe Division had been overrun, while the 246th Division and the 6th Luftwaffe Division were fighting their way west along the Vitebsk-Beshenkovichi road.

During 26 June, the 9th Corps withdrew to the Ulla River line with the remnants of the 252nd Infantry Division, Corps Detachment D, the 201st Security Division, and a collection of security and police battalions formed into Battle Group de Monteton. While these battered formations were trying to form a defensive line, the Russian attacks continued.

North of the breach on the highway between Ostrovno and Vitebsk, remnants of the 6th Luftwaffe and the 197th and 246th Infantry Divisions counterattacked with more than 1,000 men and ten to fifteen tanks and assault guns, but the attempt failed, and the survivors surrendered. The Soviets rounded up the stragglers from the 4th Luftwaffe and 246th Infantry Divisions in Ostrovno and formed a cordon to the west of Vitebsk. By noon on 27 June the Russians had taken 7,000 prisoners, and 5,000 Germans who had broken out of Vitebsk were quickly surrounded.

On 27 June the Russians made the final assault on Vitebsk, preceded by a massive barrage of artillery and rockets. By noon, the defenders had been isolated in small pockets. Small groups of Germans tried to break out of Vitebsk, but only a few survivors made their way to the ever-receding German line during the following weeks. About 8,000 broke out of the first pocket but subsequently were surrounded again and killed or captured. The Germans lost 20,000 killed at Vitebsk and 10,000 prisoners. The 4th and 6th Luftwaffe Divisions and the 206th, 246th, and 197th Infantry Divisions ceased to exist. After clearing Vitebsk, the Russians turned to the west to take part in the ongoing advance.

By 27 June, the 9th Corps had established a defense line from Uzvitsa to Lake Lukomlskoye, but it was a fragile reed—badly mauled formations, including the 252nd Infantry Division, Detachment D, the 201st Security Division, and Battle Group de Monteton. All of the units lacked the artillery and other heavy weapons that were so essential to block the advance of the Soviet armored columns.

The 212th Division promised by Hitler arrived on 27 June from the 18th Army in Latvia. It was placed between Detachment D and the 201st Security Division west of Lepel, a crucial junction where roads ran in several directions through the marshes. The dangerous hole to the south between the 3rd Panzer Army and the 4th Army was screened with Battle Group von Gottberg, made up of security and police battalions.

The 9th Corps could not hold the advancing Red Army with only two additional divisions and was forced to withdraw again, this time ten kilometers west of the Lake Lukomlskoye–Uzvitsa line. The new line ran from Gorodets (about fifty kilometers southwest of Polotsk) to Lepel and the River Essa, but because both flanks were unguarded the Soviets pressed through, threatening to envelop the 9th Corps from both north and south.

To the north the German 16th Army promised an attack from Polotsk to relieve the pressure on the north flank, but the Soviets easily repulsed the feeble attempt by three German battalions. On 28 June there were two wide-open voids, the first southwest of Lepel and the second a twelve-kilometer breach north of Gorodets between the 9th Corps and the 1st Corps of the 16th Army. By the evening of 28 June, the 9th Corps, including the remnants of the 252nd and 212th Divisions and Corps Detachment D, was strung out along the Essa River from Lepel to Gorodets.

The divisions of the 9th Corps were now badly depleted after only seven days of fighting. During the night of 27–28 June, the 252nd Infantry Division was attacked while withdrawing from Kamen, and only 300 Germans escaped. Detachment D had only forty or fifty men in its rifle battalions, many of whom were suffering foot problems from fighting and retreating in the mud and water of the marshlands for the past seven days. As many as eighty men from some battalions of Detachment D were being treated for bad feet. The 201st Security Division was removed from the 9th Corps, apparently because it was no longer an effective force. The only fresh division, the 212th, was ordered to hold the center of the 9th Corps line on the Lepel-Berezina road.

Under constant pressure, the 9th Corps withdrew again during the night of 28–29 June. Without any attacks, the overnight retreat went well for the Germans. The Soviets, however, closed up to the new positions quickly on the morning of 29 June and attacked Ushachi and Gorodets at noon. The 9th Corps was forced to retreat again to a small semicircle about seventy-five kilometers southwest of Polotsk. The corps was reduced to the remnants of the 252nd Infantry Division, Corps Detachment D, and the 212th Division. A breach over fifty kilometers wide stretched north of the 9th Corps, giving free rein to the Russians.

To the south, another seventy-kilometer gap separated the 9th Corps from the 4th Army, being driven west of the Berezina River, leaving the path open to Molodechno on 29 June. During the night the Russians took Ushachi and advanced down the Molodechno-Polotsk rail line, while the 9th Corps withdrew again to a line fifteen kilometers east of Begomli, on the Berezina River. The Germans were worn out, and many more were suffering from bad feet. Because of the continual movement some of the troops had not been fed in three days.

During 30 June the Germans fell back, closely pursued by the Soviets, who were building bridges across the Berezina River. By evening the 9th Corps held a weak position fifteen kilometers east of Glubokoye, northwest of the Polotsk-Molodechno railroad. The Russians were across the Pronia River, in the 212th Division sector, by nightfall.

On 1 July the Russians were turning the flanks of the 252nd Division as the 9th Corps retreated another fifteen kilometers to Glubokoye. In the afternoon, the Russians poured through a break north of Tumilovichi on the Berezina and struck the rear of the 212th Division. The 9th Corps had to retreat again, being pushed to the northwest and leaving the railroad to Molodechno open to the Russians in a huge gap in the German line. The 212th Division had to move north, as the forest to its rear had few roads and was infested with partisans. As a desperate blocking move, the 391st Security Division established a position on the road at Postavy about fifty kilometers west of Glubokoye, supported by the 519th Heavy Tank Destroyer Battalion, with Hornisse assault guns.

The battle had been raging for ten days, and the only reinforcements the 9th Corps had received were two divisions from Army Group North, the 252nd and 212th. The Germans deployed the 201th Security Division, but it was destroyed by 28 June. A battle group of security and police battalions evaporated within a few days. Corps Detachment D was reduced to less than a regiment. Most of the 252nd Division had been destroyed on the night of 27–28 June. The only intact units left on 1 July were the 212th Division and the 391st Security Division, which had just arrived.

From 29 June to 4 July the Soviets advanced 130 kilometers, as fast as the infantry could march. By 1 July the 3rd Panzer Army had been utterly destroyed, and the German line had been ripped apart. Gollwitzer's 53rd Corps had been eliminated at Vitebsk, and the remnant of the 9th Corps was being pushed to the northwest. The Russians now turned south to close the ring around the 4th Army at Minsk.

This narrative, with the exception of the place-names and the unit numbers, reads very much like the dissolution of the French army in June 1940 as the German panzers roamed about France. The Red Army had learned the blitzkrieg technique and applied it with a vengeance against the Germans in June 1944. Faced with the same constraint as the French in 1940, the lack of sufficient reserves, the Germans suffered their greatest defeat.

The Soviet blitzkrieg struck again south of Vitebsk with an attack on the German 6th Corps of the 3rd Panzer Army on the afternoon of 22 June. The Soviets attacked the trench lines of the first German defensive zone, held by the 197th, 299th, and 256th Divisions of the 6th Corps. The 95th and 14th Divisions were in the second zone.

One of infantry regiments of the 197th Division had been replaced by a division group of the 52nd Division. Both of these divisions should have been rebuilt in the spring of 1944. The German 256th Infantry Division had spent the entire Russian campaign in Army Group Center and, though reduced by attrition, had not suffered the catastrophic losses of many other divisions. The 299nd Infantry Division, although reduced to seven battalions in 1943, had escaped heavy losses, and its battalions were at full strength in June 1944. The division was supported by the 281st Assault Gun Brigade. The 95th Infantry Division was placed in reserve behind the 256th and 299th Infantry Divisions. The 95th, although also reduced to seven battalions, had suffered few losses in defensive fighting since 1943 and was therefore at full strength.

In addition, the 14th Infantry Division of the Army Group Center Reserve was behind the 256th Infantry Division. The 14th Division had been a motorized division, but because of the shortage of motor vehicles in 1943 and the end of German blitzkrieg advances, it had been converted to a standard infantry division in July. As a prewar regular division and former motorized division, however, the unit was of higher quality than most infantry divisions. The 6th Corps also had the 667th and 281st Assault Gun Brigades. The 6th Corps was very strong, with three good divisions on the front, two more in reserve, and the two assault gun brigades holding a forty-kilometer front. The Germans were well prepared, but the Soviet attackers overwhelmed them with artillery and tanks.

The heaviest blows fell on eighteen kilometers of the 299th Division line on the Chernitsa River. Eighty armored vehicles and 9,000 Russians attacked the thousand Germans of the 530th Regiment of the 299th Division. The Soviets broke through the German lines, and in the afternoon heavy attacks drove the 299th Division and the left flank of the 256th Division back two kilometers, forcing them out of the third trench line in the first defense zone. The 95th Division, in reserve on the Pskov-Kiev road, mounted counterattacks with the help of two regiments of the 299th Division and the 550th Penal Battalion. This counterattack gave the German frontline divisions time to occupy a second defense zone along the Luchesa River. By the evening of 22 June, the 197th German Division had been driven north to within fifteen kilometers of Vitebsk and eight kilometers west of the railroad.

To block the Soviet advance, the Germans planned a tank-supported counterattack by a regiment of the 95th Division, which was between the 197th and 299th Division on a fourteen-kilometer front on the Pskov-Kiev road. The attack failed to slow the Soviet advance, and by noon two Soviet tank columns had turned south on the Pskov-Kiev road, crossing the Luchesa River. The 299th Division retreated, and the 256th and 14th Divisions, which had arrived to help, were brushed aside as the Russians crossed the rail line leading to Orsha. The 6th Corps was broken completely in two. The 197th Division was driven toward Vitebsk and during the evening of 23 June was transferred to the 53rd Corps.

The plan for 24 June was to use the 4th Luftwaffe Division from the Vitebsk garrison to plug the hole between Vitebsk and the 6th Corps. During the morning, the remnants of the German 197th, 95th, 299th, and 256th Infantry Divisions were still holding a line about ten kilometers east of Bogushevsk, but by the end of the day the corps had been driven back to Bogushevsk under fierce attack; it was driven from the town by noon on 25 June.

The 6th Corps was cut off from the rest of the 3rd Panzer Army. By evening the gap between the 9th Corps to the north and the northern flank of the 6th Corps was thirty kilometers wide, and there were no reserves to close it. This gateway would prove to be the undoing of Army Group Center as the Soviet armored columns poured through it on the following days. The lack of three fresh divisions to shut the gate unhinged the entire Army Group Center position, and the Germans were never able to recover.

On the right flank, the 256th and 14th Infantry Divisions, facing northeast, repulsed heavy attacks northwest of Bogushevsk during the early morning of 24 June. The two divisions continued to hold the Pskov-Kiev road, giving Busch a little respite from continuous retreat.

Busch planned to pull the 4th Army back twenty-five kilometers to the Dnieper River on 25 June; together, the 3rd Panzer and 4th Armies possibly could have restored a cohesive front. Hitler approved the withdrawal of the 4th Army. However, the left flank of the 6th Corps could not hold. Fulfilling German fears, later in the morning of 25 June the Soviets overran the 299th Division and drove back the

95th at Aleksinichi, northwest of Bogushevsk. The shattered remnants of the 6th Corps, completely cut off from the 3rd Panzer Army by the breakthrough, came under the command of the 4th Army.

On 26 June the Russians exploited the breach at Bogushevsk and drove the survivors of the 6th Corps back to the south. During 27 June there were few pitched battles, but the German troops had been worn down by constant scrambling, retreating by night, digging in during the early hours of the day, waiting for the Russians, and then retreating again during the next night. There were no identifiable German units in the seventy-five kilometers between the 212th Division south of Glubokoye and the battle groups defending the flank of the 4th Army west of Borisov. The Soviet tank forces poured through this hole on their way to Molodechno, a major rail junction ninety kilometers to the west. The Russians crossed the Berezina River on 30 June and threatened the German rear at Borisov, including the 5th Panzer Division and the 14th and 95th Infantry Divisions. On 1 July the Russian mechanized units advanced rapidly, reaching Molodechno with no opposition on 2 July.

Early on the morning of 4 July the Soviets launched an attack to cross the Usha River. They were opposed by elements of the 5th Panzer Division, which included only two infantry battalions, with eighteen Pz IIIs and Pz IVs, three Tigers, three Ferdinands, eight artillery batteries, and two mortar battalions. The Russians easily overwhelmed this small force, crossed the Usha, and took Molodechno.

The first phase of the offensive in the northern sector had ended. After the fall of Molodechno, the 5th Panzer Division and additional reinforcements were able to establish a line along the River Vilnya. Army Group North had reluctantly released another division—the 170th Infantry Division was finally arriving from Narva. Even this single division made an impact, as the Russians were nearly 300 kilometers from their supply depots, at the railhead east of the start line. The wear and tear on the tracked vehicles was mounting, and a growing number were inoperable because of mechanical problems. Stocks of fuel and munitions were low; the pace of advance slowed to allow the supply trucks to come up. A round trip of four days was needed to deliver supplies. There were not enough trucks or space on the roads to provide the necessary supplies. Even slight German resistance was enough to halt the forward Russian units, which lacked stocks of munitions. By prodigious efforts on the part of the Soviet engineers, the railroads and bridges were quickly repaired, however, and the depots were being moved forward by the end of June.

The second breakthrough had been a startling Soviet success, blasting a hole in the German defenses east of Bogushevsk and driving steadily through Senno to Molodechno, where the unexpected two-week blitzkrieg ended. German reinforcements had now arrived, and the Soviet infantry and artillery were strung out far behind the armored spearheads. Given a short respite, the Germans revived and were able to begin the process of slowing down the Russian advance and withdrawing in an orderly fashion while inflicting heavy losses on the Red Army.

The third major breakthrough of the German front was at Orsha, where Stalin expected the Red Army to overwhelm two defending German divisions on 22 June and open an avenue for exploitation. The 27th Corps of the 4th Army was composed of the 78th Assault Division, the 25th Panzer Grenadier Division, and the 260th Infantry Division.

The 78th Assault Division was a unique organization in the German army, formed in January 1943 with three regiments each having a single infantry battalion, two support companies, and an artillery battalion. The divisional artillery regiment had an assault-gun battalion, an antiaircraft battalion, and a multiple-barrel mortar *(nebelwerfer)* battalion. The theory behind the formation was to provide a limited number of riflemen with a maximum amount of heavy weapons and artillery support. In June 1943 the concept was abandoned, and three infantry battalions were added to the division. The 78th Division had since become an ordinary infantry division, but the spirit of being an elite unit had persisted. On 22 June the 78th Division had an additional infantry regiment attached from the 260th Infantry Division. To the rear of the 78th Division, in the 27th Corps reserve, was the 501st Heavy Tank Battalion, located in Orsha.

The 25th Panzer Grenadier Division had been re-formed from the 25th Motorized Division in June 1943, receiving an organic tank battalion and antiaircraft battalion. With motorized infantry, the 25th Panzer Grenadier Division, of course, had greater flexibility than the marching infantry.

The 260th Infantry Division had received an additional regimental headquarters in April 1944. Many new recruits had been added during June. On 20 June, March Company 260/20 arrived from Stuttgart with 227 men, mostly returning wounded but some new men. All of the battalions had been up to strength; the new arrivals made the division overstrength. This is another indication that the Replacement

Army could have provided combat replacement battalions to rebuild the division groups while at the same time maintaining existing divisions.

The 57th Division had been sent to Kurt von Tippelskirch's 4th Army in June 1944 and assigned to a sector between the Drut and Dnieper Rivers, north of Rogachev on the south flank of the 4th Army. Because of the extremely marshy ground, the Germans correctly surmised that the possibility of a Soviet attack was very remote. The Soviet attacks developed to the north and south of the sector, and little harm was done to the German 57th Division, which was still intact on 1 July. This sector allowed the defending division to be thinned by removing a regiment for use in a more endangered area. The 199th Infantry Regiment and a battalion of the 157th Artillery Regiment were added to the 260th Division. On 18 June the 480th Infantry Regiment was attached to the 78th Assault Division, increasing to nine its number of infantry battalions.

The main blows on 22 June fell on the German 78th Assault, 25th Panzer Grenadier, and 260th Divisions. By the end of the day the 27th Corps commander doubted whether the 78th and 256th Divisions could withstand another day of massive attacks. The 260th Division had been subjected to very heavy air attacks and then artillery, and had lost many men. The division split into battle groups.

By noon on 23 June, the Russians had driven three kilometers into the German lines and repelled counterattacks by the 78th Division. The 4th Army sent forward some pitifully meager reserves to reinforce the 27th Corps: an assault gun brigade, an engineer battalion, and the 61st Security Regiment. The need was for at least two fresh divisions to solidify the second defense line and permit the battered divisions to withdraw safely. The Russians would then be forced to mount another full-scale assault against a fully alert defense line. This defensive technique had been applied repeatedly with great success in October 1943 near Kiev, costing the Red Army heavy casualties while surrendering only a few kilometers.

In the afternoon of 23 June Kurt von Tippelskirch, the 4th Army commander, requested permission to withdraw three kilometers to the second defense zone in the 78th Assault and 25th Panzer Grenadier Division sectors, as the first zone had been penetrated in many spots. Hitler denied the request and instead sent a regiment of the 14th Infantry Division to help shore up the first defense zone.

By evening the Russians had penetrated the first zone of the 78th Division and advanced nine kilometers to the second defense zone, south of Babinovichi. The Russians broke through the German defenses on the main highway to Minsk and opened a three-kilometer breach in the 78th Division line. The Russians then altered the main direction of their attack, from southwest in the direction of Orsha to due west toward Bogushevsk. By the evening of 23 June the Red Army had closed up to the German second defense zone, the Tiger line.

The Soviets resumed the attack on the 78th Assault Division and the 25th Panzer Grenadier Division during the night, giving the Germans no opportunity to consolidate their second defense line. On the morning of 24 June, OKH ordered the 27th Corps to hold and prevent any further advance toward Orsha rather than retreat to the third zone. The 27th Corps had no reserves, as the 14th Division had been sent north to help the 6th Corps south of Vitebsk. The lack of reserve divisions and Hitler's insistence on standing fast, rather than trading ground for Russian casualties, led quickly to disaster.

In the afternoon of 24 June Tippelskirch hoped to pull back his army forty kilometers to the Dnieper River. The 4th Army was still in relatively good condition, despite having given ground, and could have retreated to the river with relative ease. Only the 78th Division had sustained crippling losses. However, Hitler refused to surrender territory willingly and ordered the 260th Infantry Division on the south flank switched to the danger area in the north.

In the early afternoon of 24 June, Busch ignored Hitler's instructions and ordered a withdrawal to the Tiger line, the second defense zone, which stretched from Bogushevsk in the north to Orekhovsk, twenty kilometers northeast of Orsha, in the south. The 14th Infantry Division and a remnant of the 256th Division of the 6th Corps defended Bogushevsk on the northern flank of the army. The 256th Division had lost contact with the 6th Corps and was transferred to the 27th Corps.

Tippelskirch requested that the 78th Assault and 25th Panzer Grenadier Divisions withdraw even farther back, to the "Hessen" defense line, the third defense zone, fearing that the Russians emerging from the forest at Orekhovsk would turn south and cut off the 78th Division.

Volkers, commanding the 27th Corps, wanted to pull back on 24 June to a line three kilometers east of a line from Orekhovsk to Dubrovno, and on the next day retreat another ten kilometers to a line east of Orsha. Army Group Center still insisted that the well prepared defenses in front of Orsha be held and that only the 27th Corps should pivot back to the line Orekhovsk-Dubrovno to protect Orsha from the north. The 78th Division withdrew to the Hessen line during the evening of 24 June.

The issue at stake in the dispute was the determination of Hitler to hold prepared positions that had taken so much effort to construct. The prepared positions gave the defending Germans a decided advantage, but once a line had been penetrated they were very costly to hold. Realizing that the Russians emerging from the swamp north of Orsha were too strong to contain, the German corps and division commanders wanted to trade ground for time until reinforcements arrived. The local German commanders feared rightly that if they remained in the defenses, the Russians would destroy them.

Hitler rejected the idea of pulling the 4th Army forty kilometers back to the Dnieper River. Instead, he insisted that the fortifications east of Orsha be held. The badly mauled 78th Assault Division was ordered to maintain contact with the 3rd Panzer Army to the north—a futile command, as the interval between the armies was already over fifty kilometers wide. Rather than waiting for the Russians to overrun the German positions, Tippelskirch wanted to retreat swiftly, leaving the Russians to bombard empty trenches while the Germans prepared another line. The German generals blamed Hitler entirely for the impending disasters at Bogushevsk and Vitebsk, because he refused to permit the withdrawals.

Calamity struck during the night of 24 June, when the Soviets opened a seven-kilometer-wide hole at Orekhovsk and roared down the road leading to Orsha from the north. Two bicycle battalions of the 2nd Security Regiment were placed on the road twenty kilometers north of Orsha to stop a Russian army.

To the south the 25th Panzer Grenadier Division and the 260th Division were driven back to Orsha. The Dnieper River defense zone was ruptured, and the Russians reached Dubrovno, fifteen kilometers east of Orsha. The only available reserves were the 286th Security Division and the 342nd and 931st Security Regiments. Lacking the artillery and heavy weapons of infantry divisions, these second-rate units could not stem the Russian onslaught.

On 25 June, regardless of Hitler's orders, the 78th Division and other units of the 27th Corps retreated, and at 11 P.M., well after the fact, Hitler agreed to the withdrawals. The 25th Panzer Grenadier and 260th Infantry Divisions were ordered to pull back east kilometers east to the Hessen defense zone.

North of Orsha the situation was deteriorating rapidly on 25 June, as the German 78th Assault Division tried to maintain a link to the

25th Panzer Grenadier Division to the south. In the north the Russians turned the flank of the 4th Army; the 6th Corps of the 3rd Panzer Army was driven southward to a location west of Orsha. Soviet tanks poured through the gaping hole between the 4th Army and the 3rd Panzer Army. By the end of the day the 6th Corps had been transferred to Tippelskirch's 4th Army with the shattered remains of the 95th, 299th, 14th, and 256th Divisions. Constantly harassed by Soviet tank columns, the divisions struggled to fight their way to the rear. The 6th Corps had been torn to shreds, and a huge, sixty-kilometer hole had opened between the 4th Army and the remnants of 9th Corps of the 3rd Panzer Army.

In the south on 25 June Tippelskirch ordered the withdrawal of the 39th Panzer Corps to a position south of Orsha, halfway back from the original line, to the Dnieper River, while the 27th Corps was ordered to hold north and east of Orsha. Another fifteen-kilometer breach opened between the 78th Assault Division and the 25th Panzer Grenadier Division sector.

After fighting throughout the night, on the morning of 26 June the 27th Corps was in the second defense zone, the Tiger line. Reinforcements for the 4th Army were on the way at last; the 5th Panzer Division was moving by train from Army Group North Ukraine. However, Soviet mobile columns were running rampant, threatening the rear of Volkers's 27th Corps. The survivors of the 14th and 95th German Divisions could not stabilize the line north of Orsha, and Volkers feared that the 5th Panzer Division would be met by Russians before the tanks could be unloaded from the trains. In an attempt to create a cohesive line, the 27th Corps retreated hastily to a position southwest of Orsha. The day had been a series of disasters for the 4th Army.

On 27 June Volkers was ordered to hold the "Bear" line, the third defense zone, on the west bank of the Dnieper River south of Orsha. In addition he was ordered to fend off attacks from the north and close the gap behind Orsha. However, these tasks were all totally beyond the means of the outnumbered 27th Corps. The corps was split into three groups. South of Orsha the 39th Panzer Corps of 4th Army was also retreating to the Bear defensive zone behind the Dnieper River. Orsha was lost, and the Dnieper River line had been broken. Volkers sought permission to fight his way west. Hitler replied that the Dnieper line must be held and that if forced back, the 4th Army was to establish a new line behind the River Drut, forty kilometers west of Orsha.

The South Sector

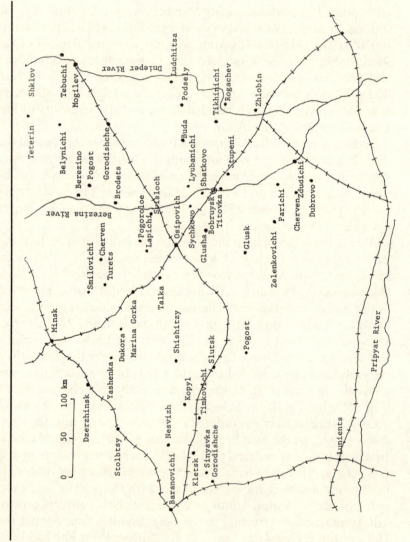

Shklov · Teterin ·

Tebuchi · Belynichi · Berezino · Pogost · Gorodishche · Brodets

Mogilev

Dnieper River

Ludchitsa · Podsely · Tikhinichi · Rogachev · Zhlobin

Berezina River

Buda · Lyubanichi · Shatkovo · Stupeni

Pogoroloe · Lapichi · Svisloch · Osipovich · Sychkovo · Glusha · Bobruysk · Titovka

Smilovichi · Cherven · Turets

Zelenkovichi · Parichi · Cherven Zdudichi · Dubrovo

Glusk

Minsk

Talka

Dukora · Marina Gorka · Shishitzy · Pogost

Yashenka

Dzerzhinsk

Stolbtsy

Baranovichi · Nesvizh · Kopyl · Timkovichi · Slutsk

Kletsk · Sinyavka · Gorodishche

Lunients

Pripyat River

100 km

50

0

On 27 June the Germans retreated to Bobr but were unable to establish a defense. The 5th Panzer Division was arriving to hold the Minsk highway, but only advance elements were at Borisov, on the south flank of Battle Group von Gottberg. Given the hopeless situation, the 27th Corps (including remnants of the 25th, 260th, 78th, and 110th Divisions) was permitted to escape early on 28 June. Hitler promised that the full 5th Panzer Division would be there within the next few days.

On 28 June 4th Army was fighting its way back, crossing the Drut River and heading for the Berezina at Borisov. The 5th Panzer Division and Battle Group Gottberg, under heavy pressure, were pushed back from Bobr to Krupki. Tippelskirch ordered his units to retreat west of the Drut. The 27th Corps was ordered to establish a line from the Drut to Chernevka, on the Berezina. Tippelskirch tried to withdraw across the Berezina River, but continuous Soviet air attacks delayed all movements. The poor secondary roads were jammed with vehicles of the service units desperately trying to escape the advancing Russians. The small bridges over the many streams that flowed through the marshes collapsed under the heavy traffic, while the major bridges over the Berezina were repeatedly damaged by bombing.

On 29 June Tippelskirch was permitted to retreat behind the Berezina River while trying to protect his flanks. Most of the troops of 4th Army had crossed the Drut River, although a considerable number were still east of the river and under heavy pressure, along with the 6th Corps, also stranded on the east bank of the Drut. By nightfall on 29 June in Minsk, only sixty kilometers west of Borisov, a horde of German service troops and stragglers from various units were out of control. The 4th Army had collapsed as remnants of its divisions struggled to cross the Berezina River, hotly pursued by the Russians. The road to Minsk was open to the Russians.

On 30 June the Germans tried to hold a bridge over the Berezina to allow the remnants of 4th Army to escape. However, Soviet tanks were in sight, coming from the north and south. The 4th Army concentrated its forces around Molodechno north of Minsk and tried to plug the hole northwest of Minsk. During the day, reinforcements arrived, including the first units of the 170th Infantry Division. With the help of the 5th Panzer Division and the 505th Tiger Battalion the Germans reopened the rail line to Minsk from Molodechno, but the Russians controlled the highway to Minsk.

Survivors of the 6th and 27th Corps had filtered back across the Berezina River throughout the day. By midnight, 20,000 German survivors were surrounded at Smilovichi. On 3 July remnants of three corps of the 4th Army were trapped on the west bank of the Berezina. The arrival of the 170th Infantry Division and the 5th Panzer Division enabled the 4th Army to establish a defense around Molodechno and delay the progress of the Red Army. Had the 4th Army received five divisions a week earlier, it might well have delayed the Russians at the Drut River line and allowed the survivors of the divisions of the 27th and 6th Corps to regroup. The arrival of even two divisions in late June had enabled the Germans to slow the Soviet advance considerably. The Soviet armies had been advancing about twenty kilometers per day for ten days and were nearly 300 kilometers from their depots. The Red Army had suffered heavily in the first few days breaking through the first German defense line, but in the following days, the Soviets broke through the unmanned second and third defense lines at comparatively little cost in men and machines.

As more fresh German divisions arrived from other fronts, the defense stiffened. Tougher resistance demanded greater quantities of munitions and more artillery, which were still stalled by traffic jams in the rear. The element of surprise so essential at the beginning of the operation was no longer available, and the battle slowed to a typical Russian campaign of costly grinding out a few kilometers per day against well prepared German positions.

The breakthrough at Orsha had been more costly to the Russians than the first two around Vitebsk, and the Soviet advance had been delayed by the need to bridge the rivers. However, Soviet pressure at Orsha had prevented the Germans from moving reserves to the north or south, and when the pincers closed, many men of the 4th German Army were taken prisoner.

The fourth major attack was launched south of Orsha with the objective of taking Mogilev and driving straight through the middle of Army Group Center. The capture of Mogilev was critical to the overall offensive. The German forces holding the sector had a high proportion of very good units that had fought tenaciously inflicting many Soviet casualties. Delayed by the 39th Corps of the 4th Army and the practically impassable terrain, the Russians at Mogilev made less progress and suffered heavier casualties than other Soviet armies in the first phase of the White Russian operation.

The 39th Panzer Corps of 4th Army, an unusually strong formation, held the center of the face of the White Russian salient. The stout resistance of this corps would inflict heavier casualties on the Red Army than any other German corps during the first two weeks of the battle to come. The corps consisted of the 12th, 31st, 110th, and 337th Infantry Divisions. In addition, the Feldherrnhalle (FH) Panzer Grenadier Division of the OKH Reserve was placed in the corps sector.

The 12th Infantry Division retained the nine-battalion structure until October 1943, when, much later than most divisions, it was reduced to seven battalions. It had not been reduced by severe losses and was well above average in strength. The 31st Infantry Division had suffered devastating losses in the retreat from Moscow in 1942 but had been lightly engaged since then and was in good condition in June 1944. The 110th Infantry Division included the 321st Division Group, as part of the program to combine understrength divisions while maintaining division and regiment traditions. The division was supported by the 185th Assault Gun Brigade. The unit had a high percentage of experienced combat soldiers and had in June 1944 probably been moved to Mogilev as the area most likely to be attacked.

The 337th Infantry Division was reinforced by the 113th Division Group, which substituted for one regiment in November 1943. The division had a high percentage of veterans and long experience on the Russian front, but because of severe losses in the past the division was the weakest in the corps and would be the first to break under Soviet attacks. Both the 110th and 337th Divisions could have been reformed in the spring with seven combat replacement battalions resulting in an additional division.

The FH Division had in June 1944 six motorized infantry battalions in two regiments, a tank battalion, and an antitank battalion. Early in June the division had provided the cadre for a new 16th Panzer Regiment for the 116th Panzer Division being organized in France, leaving the FH with only one tank battalion. The division was an elite formation in the German army, and its assignment to Mogilev along with the four other quality divisions was a testimony to the importance of Mogilev to the German defense. Their success in withstanding the Soviet attacks in most sectors of Martinek's 39th Corps for the first few days was a tribute to the quality of these five German divisions.

On 22 June Soviets attacked in the sectors of the 337th, 110th, and 12th Divisions to determine the extent of the German defenses. The attack on the 31st Infantry Division was launched to deceive the defenders as to the location of the coming major attacks. The 4th Army commander, however, saw the attacks on the 39th Panzer Corps as merely diversions. On 4th Army's south flank, the 12th Corps had little contact with the Russians.

Fog on the morning of 23 June delayed the attack by Soviet infantry in the 337th Infantry Division sector. However, the Russians smashed through the main defense zone by noon, opening a gap in the 39th Panzer Corps line. By the end of the day the Soviets had overrun all three trench lines of the main defense zone. The 337th Division was disintegrating and had lost most of its artillery. In the evening of 23 June, German counterattacks halted the Soviet advance. The FH Division was ordered to defend the 337th Division sector. In the 110th Division sector the Russians made little progress.

By the evening of 23 June, the 4th Army main defense zone had been penetrated only in the 337th Division sector. However, at 10:30 P.M. on 23 June, Tippelskirch requested permission to withdraw the 39th Panzer Corps to the second defense zone behind the Dnieper River, to shorten his line and disrupt Soviet plans for the next day. The request was denied, with an order to hold fast. In the evening the 39th Corps received three combat replacement battalions, men from the Replacement Army, including both returning wounded and new recruits. The availability of these battalions argues the possibility that the division groups could have been reconstituted.

On 24 June Tippelskirch requested but was refused permission to pull back the 12th Infantry Division, then isolated in a salient. Hitler's policy remained firm; prepared defenses were to be held as long as possible. The result was chaos when the 12th Division was driven back and could not conduct an orderly withdrawal to the next position. By late evening of 24 June, however, the resistance of the 110th Division to the north of the gap had hardened and was slowing the Soviet advance.

On 25 June four Soviet armies launched an attack on the 337th, 12th, and FH Divisions, driving them across the Basia River. The 337th Division was pushed back to the River Resta, leaving the flank of the 110th Division open. At 6 P.M. both the 12th and 31st Infantry Divisions were ordered to retreat as well to the River Resta line. Despite more German reinforcements and fierce resistance, the Russians broke through the FH Division line and reached the road to Mogilev. Tippelskirch was in serious trouble by the evening of 25 June. The 337th Division was scattered; the 110th Division was holding its own flank but could not stop the Russians; the FH Division defense line had been broken; and left flank of the 12th Infantry Division south of the FH was bending back.

To the south the 57th Infantry Division tried to maintain the tie between the 4th and 9th Armies as the 12th Corps was pushed northwest away from the 9th Army boundary. The breach that opened between the 57th Division and the 134th Division of the 9th Army allowed the Russians to unleash their armored units and threaten the rear of the German position at Bobruysk.

Because the Germans still held tenaciously on the main road into Mogilev, the Soviets shifted the weight of their attack to the north, through the swamp. The 39th Corps was on the run on 25 June. By the evening of 25 June, the German main defense zone was smashed. The survivors of the 110th Infantry Division fought their way back to the Dnieper River. The remains of the 337th Division and the FH Division desperately fought to hold open the road to Mogilev on the west bank of the Dnieper to permit others to escape. During 26 June the Soviets forced the 260th and 110th Divisions to withdraw to the Dnieper. South of Mogilev the 12th and 31st Divisions held prepared positions east of the Dnieper in the morning but finally were dislodged. The 12th Infantry Division was sent to garrison Mogilev to block the main road and rail connections. The highway through Mogilev was the only good road through the swamps and forest that separated the Drut and Berezina Rivers to the west.

Tippelskirch tried to pull all of his divisions across the Dnieper and hoped to stop the Russian advance toward Mogilev on 26 June. Because Hitler had ordered the five German divisions to hold their fortified positions, they were chewed up with no apparent gain. In addition by 26 June, the 9th Army to the south had pulled back, leaving a twenty-kilometer-wide opening between the two armies. Red Army formations pouring through the gap threatened to envelope the 4th Army. The 110th Division on the north shoulder of the Soviet penetration was driven north into 27th Corps sector.

On 27 June Hitler remained insistent that Mogilev and the single road through the marsh to Berezina be held to the last man by the 12th Infantry Division. The remaining divisions of 39th Panzer Corps fled west to the Drut. South of Mogilev, the 12th Corps retreated to Podsely.

Hitler's stubborn refusal to give ground weakened during 27 June, and he was considering pulling back the entire 4th Army across the Drut River to the west bank of the Berezina River. Tippelskirch had moved the 39th Corps part of the way back to the Drut on 27 June under constant Soviet pressure, but he worried that a retreat all the way to the Drut would turn into a rout.

During 27 June the 4th army was torn apart. No divisions were sent to reinforce it, because neither of the army groups adjoining Army Group Center were willing to part with divisions and delayed their release in spite of orders. The only hope for the 4th Army was to retreat faster than the Russians could follow. On the next day, 28 June, the 39th Panzer Corps was ordered to withdraw the remaining thirty kilometers to the west bank of the Drut. The remnants of 39th Corps crossed the Drut River and held that line. At 5:45 P.M. Tippelskirch was ordered to retreat quickly fifty kilometers west to the Berezina River, because of the disasters to the north at Orsha and to the south at Bobruysk. However, the order was too late for the 4th Army. Its divisions had been ground up trying to hold the Soviets, and the survivors were too weak to delay the pursuing Russians. After holding the Drut line for more than a day, the 39th Corps headed to the Berezina River.

South of the breakthrough in the 39th Corps sector, the 12th Corps of the 9th Army was desperately trying to escape. German engineers feverishly worked on the bridges over the Berezina River, but they were not ready until the next morning, 28 June. The 12th Corps desperately tried to delay the Russians until the next day to give the 18th Panzer Grenadier Division time to escape with its vehicles and heavy weapons. Time was running out on the 4th Army, however, and saving men soon had precedence over saving trucks and weapons.

On 29 June the most urgent task for 27th Corps, on the north flank of 4th Army, was to prevent the Russians from cutting the main escape route from the north once Tippelskirch crossed the Berezina River. The German troops reached the Berezina, but the bridges were too weak. The road to the main bridge was jammed with trucks, most of which had to be destroyed.

On the south flank of the 4th Army, 12th Corps was crossing the Drut River on the morning of 29 June. Advance elements of the Red Army reached the Berezina, opposed by elements of the 134th and 707th Divisions of the 9th Army. Half of the 12th Panzer Division arrived at 1 P.M. on 29 June to reinforce the 9th Army near Svisloch, but many units of 12th Corps were still east of the Drut. The 18th Panzer Grenadier Division could not cross until noon, after which the 267th, 57th, and 31st Divisions followed. The 4th Army had exhausted its supplies and requested airdrops of rations and ammunition. On 29 June Hitler agreed to abandon Mogilev and ordered the garrison to fight its way out, but the Russians had captured the city the previous evening.

During 30 June the FH, 12th, and 337th Divisions retreated to the Berezina River, while the 31st and 286th Security Divisions held the main road west of Berezina. The German columns waiting to cross the bridge over the Berezina were attacked by Soviet aircraft. To the south, 12th Corps was pushed farther north on the east side of the river.

On 1 July the 5th Panzer Division, the 14th Division, and some combat groups held a line on the Berezina. The 110th Division of 6th Corps was crossing the river while the 25th Panzer Grenadier Division and the 260th Division acted as the rear guard. The FH Division was trying to escape to Berezina with the remainder of the 12th Corps (the 18th Panzer Grenadier, 267th, and 57th Divisions), the 31st, 12th, and 337th Divisions, and the headquarters of the 286th Security Division. On the south flank of the 4th Army, the Minsk highway was defended by elements of the 31st, 267th, and 286th Divisions. It was all to no avail, as the Russians cut off Tippelskirch's retreat between Berezina and Cherven and headed for Minsk.

On 2 July Tippelskirch continued to pull his units across the Berezina River under heavy attacks. The 110th Division took command of all German troops crossing at Shukovets. The 12th Corps repulsed the Russian attempt to cross the Berezina River north of the village of Berezina. Still on the east side of the river were the FH Division, north of the main road, and the 18th Panzer Grenadier, 337th, and 31st Divisions south of the road.

Adding to his problems, Tippelskirch was ordered to send troops to Smolevichi to ward off the Russians attacking Minsk from the north. Tippelskirch sent units of 6th Corps to Molodechno north of Minsk to set up a defense. By the evening of 2 July, the German reinforcements had slowed the Soviet advance, but the troops left behind were rounded up by the Soviets in the following days. As the first phase of the attack on the 4th Army ended, the Germans had lost much of the elite force that had defended Mogilev. The lack of reserve divisions and the refusal of Hitler to give ground to gain time had doomed the 4th Army.

The fifth major offensive launched on 22 June was aimed at Bobruysk, defended by the German 9th Army, commanded by Gen. H. Jordan. The 9th Army would suffer a fate similar to that of the 4th Army. The Russians planned to break through at two points, envelop Bobruysk, and then press northwest toward Minsk. The German forces defending Bobruysk were stretched very thin, with slender reserves. The 12th Corps of the 4th Army, adjoining the 9th Army, consisted of the 18th Panzer Grenadier, the 267th, and the 57th Infantry Divisions. The 18th Panzer Grenadier Division had six motorized infantry battalions, an armored reconnaissance battalion, and a tank battalion. This elite and long-experienced division had superior mobility.

In the center of 12th Corps, the 267th Infantry Division held marshy ground east of the Dnieper River. The 267th Division had not suffered any unusual losses and had a high proportion of experienced soldiers. The 57th Infantry Division held a wide sector in a marshy area east of the Dnieper River, leading north to Mogilev. The division had suffered heavy losses in the Cherkassy pocket in the Ukraine in February 1944 and had been rebuilt at the Debica Training Camp in Poland in March and April. It had a high proportion of young soldiers, along with the survivors of the disaster at Cherkassy.

The three divisions of 12th Corps were more or less a screening force, covering the space between the major communication centers of Mogilev and Bobruysk. In the 4th Army reserve, the 286th Security Division could be called upon for frontline action.

The 35th Corps of the 9th Army held an extremely wide sector south of the 12th Corps covering the rail center of Bobruysk from the east. The corps included five divisions: the 6th, 45th, 134th, 296th, and 383rd Infantry Divisions, all in good condition. The 134th Infantry Division, filled with experienced soldiers and never having suffered heavy losses, held a pivotal sector; it was to be hit by the combined weight of a Soviet army and tank corps.

The 296th Infantry Division had never undergone a catastrophic defeat or lost a high proportion of its men. It held a vital sector east of the River Drut, with elements of the 45th Infantry Division in reserve. The 6th Division, although reduced by attrition, had been neither rebuilt nor combined with remnants of other divisions. The division was at full strength in June 1944 and had a high percentage of experienced soldiers. The 383rd Infantry Division had no traumatic losses and also contained a high percentage of experienced troops. The 45th Infantry Division, on the other hand, had recently been reorganized and had a high percentage of young, inexperienced soldiers. It held a sector east of the Berezina that in the event was not to be attacked by the Russians.

The 20th Panzer Division, of the army group reserve, was placed in the 35th Corps area to the rear of the 134th and 296th Division sectors, immediately in the path of the Soviet attack, which would cut off Bobruysk from the north. In June 1944 the 20th Panzer Division consisted of a single tank battalion and two panzer grenadier regiments, each with two battalions of motorized infantry. One of the infantry battalions had been replaced by recruits in April 1943, but otherwise the division had suffered from attrition rather than severe fighting. Its troops were experienced, but with only a single tank battalion of about fifty tanks, the division was no match for a Soviet tank corps. The German 707th Security Division was also in 35th Corps area in reserve near Bobruysk. It had only one artillery battalion and fewer heavy weapons than an infantry division.

The southern approach to Bobruysk was shielded by 41st Panzer Corps, consisting of the 35th, 36th, and 129th Infantry Divisions, south of the Berezina. The 35th Division had suffered no major defeats and was intact, with experienced troops.

On the north flank of General Helmuth Weidling's corps south of the Berezina River was the 36th Infantry Division, which had been reduced to a battle group after suffering crippling losses in the Orel offensive in July and August 1943. The division had since been rebuilt but had lost many of its experienced men, and the addition of a division group as a third regiment had not been a morale-building process. Accordingly, the division was below standard; unfortunately it was assigned to a sector that would receive the brunt of the Soviet attack.

On the south flank of the 41st Panzer Corps, the 129th Infantry Division had been reinforced in April 1944 by two rifle battalions from the 390th Field Training Division—another indication that combat replacement battalions were available. In June 1944 the 129th Division would be brushed aside to the south, along with the 35th Division, by the Soviet juggernaut.

The quality of 9th Army as a whole was below that of the 4th Army. The lesser quality of the divisions assigned to the army may have reflected the German high command's belief that the marshy terrain was favorable to the defenders and therefore did not require first-class divisions. In fact, three of the German divisions enjoyed strong defensive positions on the west bank of Dnieper and Drut Rivers, and the other divisions held sectors of marshland adjacent to the Berezina and Dnieper. The only major east-west road passed through Rogachev, in the securely held 296th Division sector. The Germans did not expect a major attack here.

The offensive directed at Bobruysk began a day later than the other offensives. The 9th Army sector was quiet on 22 June, the opening day of the attacks on the other armies of Army Group Center. The Germans believed that the attacks in the other sectors were ruses to divert reserves away from the south. They believed that the major objective would be Rogachev, just east of Bobruysk.

The Germans, however, would be heavily outnumbered at Bobruysk, when the attack came. Each of their regiments with at most 2,000 men was faced with a full-strength Soviet rifle division of 7,200 men. Jordan believed that the only hope was a mobile defense, trading ground for time to allow reinforcements to arrive from Army Group North Ukraine. He was especially opposed to holding fortified cities and believed that counterattacks should be launched when reinforcements arrived and the Russians outran their supplies.

On 23 June the offensive against the 9th Army began. The Russians planned to break through the first and second defense lines of the 35th Corps on the west bank of the Dnieper River and the 41st Corps sector in the south. They planned to attack after bridgeheads were secured to exploit the breakthrough with tank forces. On the north flank, at Rogachev on the Dnieper River, in the 12th Corps sector, the Soviets launched attacks on the 267th, 18th Panzer Grenadier, 35th, and 36th Divisions. It was a typical Soviet attack, by three rifle battalions with heavy artillery support. Jordan pulled a regiment from the 55th Corps and moved it behind the 35th Division, where the main attack was anticipated. Despite the shattering assault the German defenders maintained a cohesive front. The Soviets also attacked the 41st Panzer Corps line, attempting to envelope Bobruysk from the south by pressing up the south bank of the Berezina River.

On 24 June renewed heavy attacks were made on the 35th Corps. The 134th and 296th Divisions lost the first line of trenches in the morning. Late in the day the Russians overwhelmed the 296th Division and broke into the German rear. The 57th Division on the northern fringe of the attack gave way, and the Russian tanks advanced ten kilometers. The 707th Division was ordered to help. In the 41st Panzer Corps sector, the Russians pierced all five German trench lines in the first defense zone. Because of the serious nature of the breakthroughs, the 20th Panzer Division was ordered to move quickly by night to the 41st Panzer Corps area. The 20th Division, however, could not close the hole opened by the Russians between the 35th and 36th Divisions.

All during the night of 24–25 June the Soviets continued to assault the 35th Corps west of the Berezina River. In the morning of 25 June the German 36th Division was driven back, but the 20th Panzer Division arrived in the 35th Division sector. The remnants of the 35th linked up with the 129th Division of the 55th Corps, still, however, leaving in the German line a yawning gap, which had now widened to over forty kilometers. The 20th Panzer Division counterattack was futile.

The Russians continued to pound the 35th Corps at Rogachev on 25 June. The Russians drove the 36th Division back, and by 5 P.M. the 35th Division sector was falling apart. The Soviets crossed the Drut north of Rogachev. The gap between the 35th Corps and the 57th Division to the north opened to fifteen kilometers.

In the center, Jordan wanted to pull back the three German divisions (6th, 383rd, and 45th) to provide reserves to stop the Russian advances to the north and south. Jordan proposed that the entire army be pulled back to Bobruysk to save it from being encircled by Soviet pincers from the north and south. Busch refused to allow the withdrawal, on the mistaken grounds that the Russians could not move supplies through the marshland in Jordan's front and would soon be forced to halt. Busch was unaware of the capabilities of American 2.5-ton trucks provided to the Soviet Union by Lend-Lease or of how the large numbers of these trucks had bolstered the Soviet logistical system.

Jordan told Busch that the Soviets were attacking with more than 300 tanks in two tank corps, but Busch repeated the foolhardy instructions from Hitler that the line must be held. Regardless of the order, the 9th Army pulled out regiments and battalions from the divisions in the center to shore up the defense to the north and south.

By midnight of 25 June, the 35th Corps had been forced west of the Dnieper and Drut. The Russians were driving due west toward Bobruysk and threatening to cut off six German divisions (the 134th, 296th, 6th, 383rd, 45th, and 36th) in a pocket southwest of Bobruysk. The 35th Corps was disintegrating, and the 41st Corps had split in two. The entire 9th Army front was collapsing under massive attacks with a forty-kilometer breach between the 35th Division and Bobruysk to the northwest. The 35th Division was ordered to hold wherever possible. The 20th Panzer Division abandoned the 35th Infantry Division and moved north to block a Russian advance southwest of Bobruysk.

Gen. Kurt Zeitler, chief of the German General Staff, was furious that the 20th Panzer had been used, first, to help the 35th Division and now was being moved to protect Bobruysk by a roundabout route, wasting valuable time. The Germans had always used the panzer divisions as "fire departments" during Soviet offensives to seal off penetrations before they became unmanageable; in the past, reserve divisions had been available once the panzers had halted the Russians. However, there were no reserves in June 1944. Reinforcements would have to come from Army Group North Ukraine, which itself was concerned about an impending Soviet assault.

On 26 June the Red Army cut all the roads to the west and northwest of Bobruysk, including the main road to Mogilev. The Russians crossed the Berezina River, drove through the 134th and 707th German Divisions, and headed directly for Bobruysk. By noon of 26 June, the 707th German Division had been isolated and the 134th Division was under heavy attack.

The 35th Corps tried to break out to the north but was stopped. The 296th, 6th, and 45th Divisions were pushed west toward the Berezina River, and the shattered 134th Division was in flight. The Soviet armored columns were roaming freely in the German rear, having passed through holes north and south of Bobruysk. German divisions were desperately trying to escape, but most of the 20th Panzer Division and remnants of the 296th, 6th, and 45th German divisions were trapped on the east side of the Berezina. A German attack opened a railway bridge, the only avenue of escape for a mob of Germans fleeing to Bobruysk.

North of Bobruysk, the 707th and 134th Divisions were fleeing under constant attack. A Soviet armored column was closing the noose from the east; it would reach Shatkovo on the Berezina River a few kilometers north of Bobruysk on 26 June. Another Soviet tank corps cut all of the roads and bridges over the Berezina northeast and east of Bobruysk.

In the morning of 27 June, Jordan ordered the 383th Division to hold Bobruysk, while the other Germans trapped there tried to break out of the pocket in a northwesterly direction. Busch countermanded the order, demanding that all effort be made to reopen the roads but to hold the city. At 4 P.M. Hitler changed his mind and ordered Jordan to fight his way out to the northwest, leaving the 383th Division behind to hold Bobruysk—the very order that had been reversed that morning.

At 5 P.M. on 27 June, the 35th Corps turned north to link up with the 707th and 134th Divisions retreating north between the Drut and Berezina Rivers. By nightfall the 35th and 41st Panzer Corps were fleeing north on both sides of the Berezina, pursued by armored columns. Bobruysk was surrounded, and the Russians were reducing the pocket.

The 9th Army was in desperate straits in the morning of 28 June, with isolated units scattered over 150 kilometers. Most of the army, from 40,000 to 70,000 men, was trapped around Bobruysk. A wide gap stretched between the fragments of 9th army and the 2nd Army to the south, and another gap had opened between the fleeing 35th Corps and the remnants of 4th Army still holding south of Borisov.

During 28 June, because he anticipated another attack, Hitler was still reluctant to move the panzer divisions at Kovel to help the beleaguered Army Group Center. To facilitate the allocation of reserves, Hitler made Field Marshal Model commander of both Army Groups North Ukraine and Center, allowing him to decide the extent to which to weaken the Kovel area in favor of Army Group Center.

A flood of German stragglers poured into Bobruysk during the night of 27–28 June, including units of the 20th Panzer and 36th, 45th, 707th, and 134th Infantry Divisions. The German commander in Bobruysk continually requested permission from Army Group Center to break out, but the response was to leave one division in Bobruysk and allow the others to try to escape.

At noon on 28 June, the 12th Panzer Division and the 390th Training Division held a line north of Bobruysk, and most of the fresh 12th Panzer Division from Army Group North Ukraine had arrived at Marina Gorka, fifty-five kilometers south of Minsk. The 12th Panzer Division was ordered to reinforce the units on the main road to Minsk.

Finally, shortly after noon on 28 June, Hitler gave permission for all units to abandon Bobruysk. The German breakout began that night led, by the survivors of the 20th Panzer Division, with the 383rd Division. Despite Soviet efforts to reinforce the northwest sector of the ring, the Germans broke through, suffering severe losses but managing to escape. The 12th Panzer Division was able to keep the door ajar for the fleeing survivors of the 35th Corps, saving 10,000 German troops; the remaining 60,000 Germans, who had escaped from Bobruysk, were killed or captured.

The Russians were driving the survivors of the 35th and 41st Corps northwest toward Minsk and threatening to cut into the rear of the 4th Army. The units of the 12th Panzer Division were shuttled about in an attempt to halt the progress of the Soviet armored columns across a seventy-kilometer-wide gap. A battalion of the 12th Panzer Division attacked Svisloch, trying to rescue about 35,000 men moving north out of Bobruysk. Although the attack was beaten off, about 15,000 unarmed Germans were able to cross the river during the day and walk to Marina Gorka, fifty kilometers to the west, within the next few days; there they boarded trains for Minsk and beyond. (The railroads could move large numbers of men even in the chaotic situation of late June.) At midnight on 29–30 June, Hitler designated Minsk a "fortress city" and appointed a commander with orders to defend it to the end. In preparation, the 9th Army was ordered to fortify the city. At that time, there were only 1,800 stragglers and some limited-service men there.

Model abandoned any hope of holding Minsk on 1 July and ordered Jordan to withdraw to the edge of the Nalibotski Forest between Stolbtsy and Molodechno. On 2 July the 390th Training Division with six security battalions tried to hold a line south of Minsk but was driven back. In Minsk, fifty-three trains were stranded when the rail lines to the west were cut. The 15,000 German stragglers on the trains refused to help defend the city.

On the night of 2–3 July, the 12th Panzer Division set off for Stolbtsy. The bad roads were clogged with hundreds of Germans fleeing on foot. Some of the refugees were picked up as replacements for the division. By 3 July the 9th Army, which had held the sector east of Bobruysk, had been reduced to prisoners in Soviet camps or unarmed stragglers desperate to escape. Model abandoned Minsk and concentrated his forces to delay the Soviet drive southwest toward the rail center at Baranovichi. The destruction of the 9th Army was a devastating loss, leaving a massive breach in the German line in central Russia.

Logistics, as elsewhere, finally caught up with the Russians, but the arrival of German reinforcements was the primary cause for the pause in the offensive. Moving ammunition forward to fight the fresh German divisions placed an additional strain on the Soviet logistical system.

As supplies arrived the attack resumed but at a slower pace, against increasing German resistance. In the days following the battle for Bobruysk, the Russians would clean up numerous pockets of

Germans east of Minsk and regroup to begin the second phase of the operation.

The final attack of the six Russian offensives against Army Group Center was launched in the southeast corner of the White Russian salient. The mission of the Soviet armies there was to break through the 55th and the 41st Corps of the 9th Army, then race west to Slutsk and Baranovichi and block the route of German reinforcements from Kovel. This task could have been accomplished more profitably by using the 5th Guards Tank Army to attack farther west at Luninets, along the rail line leading to Baranovichi. The tank army would then have encountered very weak resistance and possibly cut the tie between Army Group Center and the North Ukraine Army Group.

The south shoulder of the White Russian salient was held by the 55th Corps of the 9th Army and Weiss's 2nd Army. Only Herrlein's 55th Corps was attacked in the opening days of the offensive; the 2nd Army front was quiet. The 55th Corps held a wide sector with only two divisions. The 292nd Infantry Division was on the east flank bordering on the 41st Panzer Corps. Because the division had not suffered serious losses, the troops were well seasoned, with a minimum number of young soldiers.

The 102nd Infantry Division, which held the west half of the 55th Corps sector, was reinforced by the 216th Division Group, which had replaced the 233rd Infantry Regiment in November 1943.

The 2nd Army held more than 300 kilometers of the south shoulder of the White Russian salient that ran through the Pripyat Marsh. Nearly half of the sector was held by the 23rd Corps, with the 203rd Security Division on the east and the 7th Infantry Division on the west. The 7th Infantry Division had suffered devastating losses in the Orel operation in late 1943. The 203rd Security Division included two three-battalion security regiments, a single artillery battalion, and some Russian POW units. All German security units were composed of older men with a minimum of heavy weapons; they were meant to fight partisans. Both divisions merely provided a screen to prevent intrusion by small Soviet units; the ground was too wet for major operations. The corps reserve consisted of the 1st Hungarian Cavalry Division and the 17th Special Brigade, with three security battalions.

West of the 23rd Corps, the 20th Corps held another wide sector with the 3rd Cavalry Brigade and Corps Detachment E. The 3rd Cavalry Brigade included a cavalry regiment with three battalions, an artillery battalion, an assault-gun battalion, a heavy weapons battalion, and a Cossack battalion. The brigade was stretched over a sixty-kilometer sector, forming a thin screen.

Corps Detachment E was a division-sized unit of remnants of the 86th, 137th, and 251st Infantry Divisions. It was assigned the low-risk duty of screening a sixty-kilometer sector in the Pripyat Marsh. The corps reserve included the 4th Cavalry Brigade.

The 8th Corps held the narrowest sector on the east end of the 2nd Army, with its southern flank only forty kilometers from Kovel. The corps included the 12th Hungarian Reserve Division, the 211th Infantry Division, and the 5th Jäger Division. The 12th Hungarian Reserve Division had been added to the corps recently to screen the less-sensitive eastern part of the corps sector. Because the Hungarian units did not fight well in Russia, they were usually confined to security duty, fighting the partisans. However, the need to bolster the defense near Kovel probably led to the addition of the Hungarians to concentrate the remaining divisions in the west sector.

The 211th Infantry Division, holding a twenty-kilometer sector, had been rebuilt with remnants of the 321st Infantry Division in the fall of 1943 after being mauled in battles around Bryansk in July 1943. The unit's assignment to a significant sector indicates that the German high command had confidence in the division.

The 5th Jäger Division, with specialized training, had not suffered severe losses since 1941 and was probably better than average. The 904th Assault Gun Brigade, with sixty assault guns, was attached, and the corps reserve, the 237th Assault Gun Brigade, was stationed immediately behind the division, giving it a powerful armored component equal to a panzer division.

Deep in the 2nd Army reserve, under the 2nd Hungarian Reserve Corps, were the 23rd and 5th Hungarian Reserve Divisions, fighting partisans. The Hungarians lacked frontline combat experience. Overall, the 2nd Army was a weak force; its task was to screen the Pripyat Marsh to prevent Soviet raids. The 2nd Army had few resources available to help its neighbors to the north.

On the first two days of the battle, 22 and 23 June, the Russians attacked the flank of the German 35th and 129th Divisions, driving them toward the railroad south of Bobruysk. On 25 June the Russians broke the line of the 35th and 129th Divisions in five places. Having sent most of its battalions north to help the other divisions of the 41st Corps, the 129th Division was reduced to regimental level. During the day, the 129th Division was forced to retreat, leaving a gap on the north flank of the 55th Corps. A group of three training battalions was formed to hold the gap between the 129th Division and remnants of the 35th, again evidence that there were battalions available to upgrade the division groups. These battalions would have been much more effective in divisions with experienced noncoms, standard allotments of heavy weapons, and artillery support.

The 292nd Division was forced to withdraw to keep in contact with the north. At 4 P.M. on 25 June, Busch, the army group commander, ordered the division to hold, to bend back only on the north flank. The 35th Division was scattered, and the remnants were forced to retreat to the west, further widening the gap south of the 36th Division. The Russians had cut all roads south and southwest of Bobruysk and crossed the railroad south of Bobruysk by the evening of 26 June. The 129th Division, south of the 35th Division, was also forced to retreat to protect the northern flank of the 55th Corps.

On 26 June the Soviets forced the 35th Division back to the Ptich River west of the railroad, creating a forty-kilometer breach between the division and the 36th Division to the north. The Germans were ordered to hold wherever possible, but there were no reserves to fill the breach north of the 35th Division. The same day, the 55th Corps held a line on the River Ptich, but the Russians already had crossed the river to the north, threatening to outflank the 35th and 129th Divisions. The Russians headed due west for Slutsk and cut the Mogilev-Slutsk railroad. The 129th and 292nd Divisions of the 55th Corps continued to hold the Ptich River line, under moderate pressure. On 27 June the divisions were ordered to pull back from the river to avoid being cut off from the north.

By the evening of 28 June the Russians brushed aside two German battle groups defending Slutsk on the main road from Bobruysk to Baranovichi, which was the rail terminus for the incoming German divisions from the south.

The 2nd Army on the Pripyat River was not under pressure from the Soviets. However, as the Russians advanced across its rear to the north, Weiss had to make adjustments to protect his flank. The 9th Army weapons training school and a German cavalry regiment were trying to stop the Soviets east of Slutsk. Weiss was ordered to pull back the 23rd Corps to maintain a link with the 9th Army. Weiss began to thin out his line in order to send units north to help the 9th Army. The first to be dispatched was the 1st Hungarian Cavalry Division, the army reserve.

Although most of the Army Group Center was in difficulty, the 55th Corps was stable, with little pressure from the Russians. The three divisions of the corps (the 129th, 292nd, and 102nd Infantry Divisions) retreated thirty kilometers on 29 June in an attempt to protect the corps's northern flank. The gap between the 55th Corps and the Germans at Slutsk had widened to sixty kilometers. However, help was on the way. On 29 June the first three trains of the 4th Panzer Division arrived in Baranovichi, ninety kilometers west of Slutsk; the 28th Light Division as well as the 7th Panzer Division were ordered to follow.

On the 29th only a string of isolated German units remained at Slutsk, under the command of the 1st Cavalry Corps. On 30 June the Russians took Slutsk, but the first units of the 4th Panzer Division arrived in Baranovichi and blocked the main road west of Slutsk. The 1st Hungarian Cavalry Division from the 2nd Army was on its way to Baranovichi. The 28th Division was in transit; it would arrive the next day at Dzerzhinsk, halfway between Minsk and Stolbtsy.

To the south, the 129th Division of the 55th Corps and the remnant of the 35th Division pulled back nearly fifty kilometers. The other two divisions of the corps, the 292nd and 102nd, slowly retreated, keeping contact with the 129th Division.

On 1 July the 6th Cavalry Brigade delayed the advancing Russians. The first three battalions of the 28th Light Division were to unload at Stolbtsy, on the rail line from Baranovichi to Minsk, and defend the town. However, the arrival of the 28th Division was delayed nearly a day by sabotage of the railroad by partisans.

The Russians captured the railroad bridge at Stolbtsy, cutting the rail line to Minsk, and continued to advance early on the morning of 2 July. The 4th Panzer Division and the 1st Hungarian Cavalry Division were ordered to counterattack but were delayed because they lacked fuel, an indication of partisan success in disrupting rail traffic.

During the evening of 2 July, the 12th Panzer Division was ordered to move to Stolbtsy along with attached combat groups, in effect abandoning the road to Minsk from Bobruysk to the Russians. On 3 July all the rail and road connections were cut between Stolbtsy and Baranovichi. Elements of the 20th Panzer Division and remnants of many other units fought their way northwest along the Neman River. German engineers built a bridge across the Neman about thirty kilometers northwest of Stolbtsy; it served as an escape route for thousands of Germans fleeing Minsk. Throughout the night, stragglers crossed the bridge and fought their way southwest to Baranovichi.

A counterattack by the 4th Panzer Division from Baranovichi went well on the morning of 3 July. Also, more reinforcements were arriving; thirteen trains carrying the 28th Light Division arrived at Baranovichi during 3 July. German reinforcements had stabilized the front around Baranovichi and, by 3 July, rescued 25,000 men who had fled from the Bobruysk area.

From 22 June to 3 July the Russians had forced the Germans in the southeast corner of the White Russia salient to retreat 250 kilometers to Stolbtsy. After the initial breakthrough, the Soviets advanced an average of twenty kilometers per day. The German 2nd Army and the 55th Corps were forced to withdraw to protect their flanks. On 3 July German and Hungarian units at Stolbtsy finally halted the Russian armored columns, which lacked power and supplies to overcome the increasing German resistance; the Russians had to pause until the infantry, artillery, and supplies caught up to the armored spearheads. The progress of the Russians finally ground to a halt on the southern flank, and the blitzkrieg phase of the campaign against Army Group Center ended. During the following days, a small but steady stream of German units arrived to slow the Soviet advance and force the Russians to resume the costly battles of attrition.

Had the Germans formed an additional sixty divisions in the spring of 1944 as might have been expected, there would have been at least a dozen divisions available to Army Group Center in June when the attack began. The early commitment of these divisions would have blunted the Soviet onslaught and prevented the costly encirclements that led to the capture of many German troops.

The Russians, as well, had made in their planning a serious error that stalled their attack when they reached Baranovichi. They should have launched an additional attack on the southern flank of the White Russian salient at Luninets, with the 5th Guards Tank Army. A rail line leading through Luninets to Baranovichi offered a good passage through the marshes, and attacking Russians would have faced little opposition. The Soviet tanks would have delayed the arriving German divisions until the remainder of the Red Army had destroyed Army Group Center. By inserting the 5th Guards Tank Army in the south rather than in the center, a huge amount of rail traffic would have been diverted to the line passing through Gomel instead of the overburdened line passing through Smolensk, which as it was delayed the offensive by at least seven days. Given the change in the deployment of Gen. Pavel Rotmistrov's army, the original timetable would have been possible and the offensive launched in mid-June, before the rains came. The Pripyat Marshes would have been less daunting than the swollen Drut and Berezina Rivers after the rain in late June.

The 5th Guards Tank Army was not needed at Orsha and could have been replaced by a more agile horse-mechanized group; the 1st White Russian Front had enough units in reserve to form two horse-mechanized groups. The success of the other two cavalry groups was a result of their greater mobility. For instance, a thirty-ton pontoon bridge was sufficient for a cavalry group, whereas a tank army required sixty-ton pontoon bridges, the most troublesome part of the tank army support element. The poor performance of the 5th Guards Tank Army, resulting from its difficulty in bridging the Drut and Berezina Rivers, was noted by the Soviet command.

Regardless of the missed opportunity offered by a Soviet strike in the south, within a few days after 22 June the German defenses were broken and Soviet armored columns ranged widely and deeply. Late in the first phase, Rotmistrov's 5th Guards Tank Army advanced 125 kilometers in three days, from 26 June to 28 June, and the 2nd Mechanized Brigade of the 3rd Guards Mechanized Corps advanced seventy kilometers. Had the Germans at Kursk in July 1943 averaged twenty kilometers per day from the north and south (a total of forty kilometers per day to close a 200-kilometer gap), they would have closed the trap in five days and surrounded the Soviet armies in the salient before the latter's reserves could arrive.

From 4 July to 16 July, after the accelerated first phase of the White Russian operation, the Russians continued to advance, although at a slower pace. Army Group Center received reinforcements from the OKH reserve, Army Group North Ukraine, and Army Group South Ukraine. By 17 July the Germans had reestablished a front and slowed Soviet progress to as little as a kilometer per day.

The calculated restriction of movement of troops from the Replacement Army very likely added to the devastating impact of the surprise attack of 22 June, which gave the Russians the long-sought prize of Vitebsk and a huge bag of prisoners at comparatively small cost in men and weapons. However, the brief interlude of blitzkrieg came to an end, and the pace slowed to the all-too-familiar rhythm of the Russian front once German reserves arrived in August and the surprise effect of the Soviet assault had worn off. The Russians were once again faced with pushing ahead in slow motion in a costly war of attrition.⌡

The Red Army inflicted a staggering defeat on the German army in White Russia. The psychological culmination of the Soviet victory was the parade of 57,000 German prisoners through the streets of Moscow, the only such event during the war.

8
Conclusion

The Americans, the British, and the Russians, as well as the German populace, owe a debt of gratitude to the men who plotted to kill Hitler in July 1944. Although the outcome was not as they intended, the capture of 765,000 German soldiers in July and August 1944 did shorten the war. Fortunately for them, most of these men returned to Germany after the war rather than losing their lives in a futile last-ditch effort to win it.

On 1 July 1944 the German army had 892,000 men in the West and 2,160,000 on the Eastern Front. In the West the Germans suffered nearly 400,000 permanent losses, 54,754 dead, and 338,933 missing from June to September 1944. On the Eastern Front in the same period the Germans lost more than 700,000—191,400 killed and 516,200 missing. The total permanent German loss on the two fronts was 901,200 men, of whom 855,000 were missing, presumed prisoners (see Table 8.1).

The German army suffered more permanent losses in two months, July and August 1944, than in the twelve-month period ending May 1944. The number killed in these two months was about half of those lost in the prior six months, or double the monthly average.

Table 8.1
Permanent Losses in All Areas, June to August 1944

Month	Killed	Missing	Total
June 1944	26,000	32,000	58,000
July 1944	59,000	310,000	369,000
August 1944	64,000	407,640	471,640
September 1944	42,400	67,200	109,600
Total June through September 1944	191,400	816,840	1,008,240
October 1944	46,000	79,200	125,200
November 1944	31,865	69,534	101,399

The number missing was three times the total of the previous twelve months, and sixteen times the monthly average of the previous year—a catastrophe!

In perspective, the United States lost 405,399 killed in all theaters in the Second World War, and of those only 291,557 were combat related.

Why did the Germans lose so many prisoners in June and July 1944 (reported in July and August, the respective months following the losses)? The number is astonishing, compared to only 127,000 reported missing in January 1943, following the debacle at Stalingrad. Such heavy losses on two fronts cannot be mere coincidence.

As a skeptic, I do not believe in coincidence, which is often invoked as cover stories explaining covert action. We know there was a conspiracy, but we do not know the extent of what was done. The thesis presented is that much more was involved than is commonly known, especially with respect to the Replacement Army.

A curious series of events occurred on 17 July. In the morning Rommel sent a message to Hitler pointing out that only 10,000 replacements had arrived in the previous weeks compared to 110,000 losses; this dispatch would have alerted Hitler to the actions of the Replacement Army. There is some question, however, as to whether this message was ever delivered. At 6 P.M., as Rommel was driven to the front (or to Germany—there are conflicting accounts), two British fighters attacked Rommel's car in an attempt to kill him. I cannot recall seeing in the succeeding fifty-seven years any explanation of why two British fighters were in the American sector attacking road traffic, a task normally performed by P-47s of the Ninth Air Force. Nor can I recall any mention of the names of the pilots or of their squadron. Rommel commanded from the front and was aware of the risks of air attack. That he would have knowingly exposed himself to such an attack is not at all likely.

The details of July 1944 plot and the cooperation of British intelligence will probably never be known. Many documents remain classified in the Public Record Office in London. Still unavailable is information on Soviet and German units during World War II gathered for British intelligence by thousands of clerks directed by Professor Eric Birley. In 1975, *German Order of Battle 1944* was published, purporting to be an exact copy of the British army reference work prepared in June 1944 by Birley's organization for use by intelligence officers. However, internal evidence clearly indicates that the report reflected the situation as of 1 November 1943. The date is significant—it means that the report ignores the activity of the Replacement Army in the crucial months from November 1943 to June 1944. In my visits to the Public Record Office, I found no references to reports for those months. As one British intelligence officer adroitly puts it, to reveal the data is to reveal the source.

That the details are not known is perhaps just as well, but it is important to be aware that the astonishing victories on both the Eastern and Western Fronts in July and August 1944 were not solely the result of the brilliance of Allied commanders. For instance, one Allied attack preceded by a massive air attack destroyed the Panzer Lehr Division, but that division already had been reduced to a shadow. In the few days before Cobra, the division lost 350 men, yet in the entire period from the invasion to 25 July it had received only 200 replacements. Even in quiet sectors, most divisions received an average of 500 replacements per month! Yet in Germany there were 400 combat replacement battalions in the Replacement Army, with roughly 800 to 1,000 men each, awaiting orders.

Had the Allies indeed vanquished the German army in July and August, in the succeeding months German monthly losses should have remained fairly constant, rather than dropping from 475,000 killed and missing in August to only 110,000 in September. In September, October, and November 1944 the number killed in action remained at 40,000 or less, indicating that intensive fighting was continuing.

However, German losses of prisoners decreased dramatically, from 400,000 in August to 67,000 in September, a clear indication that the German army was no longer on the run but had stabilized the fronts. The reason for the dramatic change was the arrival from Germany of fresh divisions previously held back by the Replacement Army.

The lack of new divisions and replacements in 1944 was not a co-incidence but a deliberate program to delay the transfer of new men to the field army. Still in question is whether all of those involved in the plot were aware of the intention to hold 600,000 men in the Replacement Army, deny replacements to the divisions in combat, and postpone the formation of new divisions that would have provided a strategic reserve. Not all of the conspirators knew of the actions of the Replacement Army. Those who held the men in Germany did so with considerable skill, to avert detection. However, the end result was obvious to the frontline commanders.

The statistical evidence is compelling. Even after the formation of nearly sixty divisions in August and September 1944, the Replacement Army was still overflowing compared to previous years. The program of slowing the release of men from the Replacement Army probably began as early as October 1943 (see Table 8.2).

While the number of men in the field army was shrinking, the number in the Replacement Army was increasing (see Table 8.3).

The additional 210,000 men in the Replacement Army in 1944 were adequate to form twenty-four divisions. The additional 830,000 men in other organizations reflected the increase in SS and parachute divisions. The men in the Replacement Army in the spring of 1944 were well trained, and many had combat experience. From 1 June 1943 to 31 May 1944, 2,645,000 men were inducted into the armed forces. The average was approximately 210,000 per month. Therefore,

Table 8.2
Men in the Replacement Army

August 1939	996,000
1941	1,243,000
1942	1,800,000
October 1943	2,300,000
October 1944	2,336,000

Table 8.3
Comparison of the Field Army and the Replacement Army

	1943	1944
Field army	4,250,000	4,000,000
Replacement Army	2,300,000	2,510,000
Other	4,730,000	5,560,000
Total armed forces	11,280,000	12,070,000

only a small percentage of the Replacement Army consisted of new inductees with less than eight weeks' training.

The very composition of the Replacement Army reveals a movement to conceal the available replacements in other organizations within the army. The composition of the Replacement Army in July 1944 indicated an extremely unlikely situation. There were an unusually large number of men classified as recovering wounded or in hospitals, although in previous months there had been only limited operations on the Russian front and in Italy (see Table 8.4).

The 500,000 recruits training was more than double the average number of inductees per month, whereas one would expect that each month 200,000 recruits would complete their training as 200,000 new recruits arrived. In 1944, few recruits needed more than eight weeks' training, and many required less, having had prior military service. At least 100,000 men were falsely classified as recruits in training.

The 600,000 men in the march battalions and recovered-wounded companies accounted for most of the surplus in the Replacement

Table 8.4
Composition of the Replacement Army, July 1944

March battalions ready for combat	400,000
Recruits training	500,000
Recovered wounded companies	200,000
Training personnel, school troops	230,000
Men in hospitals	700,000
Landesschutzen battalions	300,000
Total	2,500,000

Army. These men would have been enough to fill the proposed sixty divisions. Even though nearly sixty divisions were formed in August and September, absorbing at least 7,000 men per division, in October 1944 the total manpower in the Replacement Army was still 2,336,000. These numbers refute the argument that inadequate manpower was available in early 1944 to form new divisions or provide replacements for the field army. Nor can one argue that the new divisions would not have been trained or experienced. Of the 600,000 men in march battalions and recovered-wounded companies available on 1 July 1944, one-third obviously had combat experience—they had the wounds to prove it. Few if any of the American divisions that landed in France in 1944 had that proportion of personnel with combat experience.

What steps could have been taken had the 600,000 men not been held back in the Replacement Army? The same program that had been carried out in the summer of 1941, 1942, and 1943 could have created sixty "new" divisions by June 1944. The new divisions could have been formed from existing elements, just as new divisions had been formed in previous years.

The most common technique was the upgrading of occupation divisions in France by replacing overage, unfit men with new recruits and replacing captured weapons with German equipment. This ritual occurred annually in France in 1941, 1942, and 1943, but not, as we have seen, in the spring of 1944. The upgrading and rebuilding program that began in France in November 1943 was nearing completion by February 1944, and very little was accomplished after that.

More occupation divisions in France could have been upgraded in a few weeks by sending seven combat replacement battalions to each—a total of 200 battalions with 200,000 men, half of whom would have been experienced soldiers returning to action after recovery from wounds, the other half recently trained recruits. The seven battalions would have replaced most of the men in each occupation division, and the Ost battalion would have provided service personnel. The older men replaced could have been formed into new fortress brigades of four battalions. The fortress brigades could have remained where they had been for three or four years, armed with the emplaced artillery and heavy weapons. The newly upgraded division would have been available as a reserve. The result would have been twenty-eight infantry divisions available to be moved into the Normandy beachhead. The existence of such a reserve would have created second thoughts about launching the second front and might well have delayed it another year, adding to the misery of the German people as the bombing continued.

In the East, a similar group of 200 combat replacement battalions could have been dispatched to reconstitute the division groups, regiment-sized units that represented the combat elements of a division reduced by combat losses in 1943. The rear elements of some of these divisions had been sent to France to form new divisions in late 1943. Sixteen of the division groups were in the eight corps detachments, division-sized units with the rear element of one battered division, one or two of the division's infantry regiments, and one or two division groups from other divisions. The eight corps detachments could have formed twenty-four reconstituted divisions in a short time by the addition of seven combat replacement battalions for each division. Additional service troops were available from Soviet prisoner of war camps and from service troops combed from other divisions as the service elements were reduced under new tables of organization in 1944. Additional division groups were assigned to other divisions in place of a third infantry regiment, and these could have been reconstituted, for a total of thirty-two new divisions.

The presence of thirty-two infantry divisions in reserve in June 1944 would have mitigated the disaster in Army Group Center, reducing considerably the capture of thousands of German soldiers. They had been surrounded trying to hold fortified lines because there was no occupied second line of defense behind them.

Even the dispatch of 400,000 men in 400 combat replacement battalions would have left 200,000 men available over and above the normal strength of the Replacement Army. These men could have provided a field replacement battalion to each new division and 140 additional combat replacement battalions to be held in readiness in the East and West to replace losses quickly. The Replacement Army would merely have been reduced to its normal strength.

That such a program was possible is clearly indicated by the creation of fifty-four new divisions in late July and August of 1944, when Hitler was again in control. There is no apparent reason why that program could not have been launched in March or April 1944 had not the staff of the Replacement Army refused to release the battalions before 20 July 1944. Once those who had held back the troops in Germany were removed, the Replacement Army quickly formed new divisions and filled depleted ones. The German army in September, even after the loss of 845,000 men in the previous two months, was strong enough to halt or impede Allied advances in both East and West.

That the German army should suffer more losses, primarily prisoners, in July and August of 1944 than in any other two months of the war and then have a miraculous renewal of strength in September cannot be explained as a coincidence or as a fortuitous combination of circumstances that disappeared without apparent cause. The ability of Germany to cope with large-scale offensives on several fronts in Russia had been proven time and again. If the combined forces of the British, Americans, and Russians had reached such a level in July and August that German resistance was unable to forestall the catastrophes that occurred in both East and West, why was the German army able to contain both fronts in September, even though the opposing armies were growing steadily in strength? The Allied and Soviet armies continued to advance in the next eight months, but they did so at enormous cost to themselves and at comparatively low cost to the Germans.

The reason for the lack of the usual flow of new units, replacements, and new equipment to the fronts from Germany was that the leaders of the coup that attempted to kill Hitler were retaining units and equipment in Germany to be used after the assassination to take control of Germany from the Nazi Party. The generals assumed that the SS would remain loyal to the Nazi Party leaders and would have to be subdued. In addition, as Hitler was an extremely popular leader, the assumption was that troops would be necessary to control a reaction by the civilian population. To carry out the carefully planned coup, the conspirators needed a large number of trained army units to take the German cities and towns from the Nazis.

Therefore, the system was abruptly halted at a time when troops and weapons were sorely needed to prepare new divisions for the anticipated attacks on both fronts. Even the handful of divisions that were transferred from other army groups were able to halt the Soviet offensive in White Russia by August 1944. In the West, and although Patton claimed to have logistical problems, only a few German divisions were able to halt his drive in September. Hitler acknowledged after the plotters finally had been eradicated that once again the troops and equipment were flowing to the fronts; had the units retained in Germany been formed into divisions as had been the established practice and sent to the front in July, they might well have been enough to reduce the scale of German losses, which would have prolonged the war for many months.

Since 1941 the existence of a strategic reserve of fresh divisions had proved to be essential to both offensive and defensive battles in the East. These fresh divisions were added to a sector either to provide local superiority for an offensive or the means to stop an enemy offensive. France was the training ground for the strategic reserve, beginning in June 1941. The availability of groups of new or rebuilt divisions about every six months gave the German high command a strong hand in determining the activity on the Eastern Front. With the knowledge that the second front would come in France in May or June 1944, in November 1943 Hitler ordered that new and reformed divisions remain in the West. No further divisions were transferred from France to the East after November 1943, depriving the Germans of the strategic initiative there. Although creation of new divisions continued, the Replacement Army held back enough troops to create and maintain a powerful force of battalions in Germany that would obey army (rather than party) orders once Hitler was removed.

Without new units, the German army on the Eastern Front had few reserves in the summer of 1944, a lack that led to the destruction of Army Group Center in June. Neither East nor West had adequate forces to withstand the attacks that came in June 1944, and few additional forces arrived from Germany. The carefully planned, not coincidental, delay in movement of new units from Germany to France and Russia in June and July exacerbated the situation on both fronts and hampered the efforts to re-create fronts after Allied and Soviet breakthroughs.

With the removal of the plotters and the resumption of the flow of men and material to the fronts, the German army was able to stop the Western Allies at the German border and delay the advance of the Soviets in September 1944. It was neither the failure of the American supply service nor the fact that the Russians were far from their depots in early July that halted their respective advances but the arrival of fresh German divisions. After the removal of the plotters from command positions, a massive number of new divisions were created in a few short months from the ample supply of manpower previously held back. The culmination of this rebuilding effort was the assembly of two panzer armies that dealt the Americans a stunning blow in the Ardennes in December 1944.

Many readers will question the thesis that the Germans could have created a strategic reserve of sixty divisions in the spring of 1944. I suggest answers to some of the most obvious challenges.

First, had the Germans ever created such a large number of divisions in so short a time? In the months preceding the attack on Poland and again in the months preceding the invasion of Russia in June 1941, large numbers of divisions were formed. Between January 1942 and May 1942, the Germans formed the Seventeenth, Eighteenth, and Nineteenth Waves, as well as seventeen new and refitted divisions.

Were enough men available to carry out the program suggested here? Hitler's directive ordering 1,000,000 men to the front in November 1943 resulted in a surplus of at least 600,000 men in the Replacement Army in the spring of 1944. The surplus remained until August, when some of the men formed over fifty divisions in August and September 1944.

Where would the cadre for the divisions have come from? The program outlined suggests the reconstitution of existing units to mobile infantry division status. Occupation, reserve, and field training divisions already had division structures. The division groups had regimental structures but the traditions of divisions. Finding majors and colonels worthy of promotion would not have been difficult. The returning wounded included a vast pool of noncoms. Germany had been at war for more than four years and had many experienced soldiers.

Were adequate weapons available? Albert Speer's reorganization of the armament industry was in full swing by the spring of 1944. There was no difficulty in the fall of 1944 in finding weapons for the new divisions formed then, including new assault rifles. A possible shortage of divisional artillery pieces could have been alleviated by the use of captured guns and 88 mm antiaircraft guns.

Where would the Germans have found the additional trucks and horses needed? The French economy was still a source of both trucks and horses. Confiscation of French equipment would have occurred in any case, once the Allies landed in Normandy.

Even had the divisions been reconstituted, could they have been moved to the front? The German and French railways were functioning well in 1944, as were the lines used by the Germans in Russia. Many of the divisions would have been rebuilt either in the rear of the army groups in Russia or in French training camps. There were few problems in transportation as shown in examples in previous chapters.

Had the men been used to form new divisions, there would have been none left over for replacements! To the contrary—if 600,000 men had been taken from the Replacement Army in the spring of 1944, more than a million men would have remained, including the average number usually in training and recovering from wounds.

Reconstituting divisions took much longer than two months! As outlined in examples above, the Replacement Army assembled divisions in a matter of weeks, because of the large number of experienced men available among the returning wounded and those combed out of service units. The author had personal experience in reconstituting the U.S. 38th Infantry Regiment in 1946. Given a cadre of veterans, only a few weeks were needed to rebuild rifle companies from recruits fresh from basic training.

Where would the headquarters, service, and artillery units have come from? The occupation, reserve, and field training divisions had headquarters units. The service units could have been formed from men taken from service units of other divisions early in 1944. The artillery battalions could have been created with cadres from other divisions and recruits from artillery replacement battalions. Even the divisions that had three rather than four artillery battalions in the beginning were still more combat worthy than the scratch units used in the fighting in Normandy and White Russia.

Where would the officers and noncoms have come from? Germany had been at war for more than four years, and many field-grade officers were probably long overdue for promotion, as few officers of that rank became casualties. Company-grade officers would have been in short supply, but two officers per company, one in the rear and one at the front, were adequate. Platoons were usually commanded in combat by sergeants in all armies in World War II.

Would not these new divisions have been of poor quality? Compared to Soviet divisions that acquired replacements from partisan units or by drafting men from recaptured cities, the German manpower would have been well trained. Few American divisions had any combat experience, but they learned quickly. So would have the new German divisions.

Why was Hitler unaware of the unusual expansion of the *Valkure* force? His health had deteriorated in early 1944, and he was no longer able to assimilate the mass of detail that had been his strength in previous years. The explosion of the bomb cured the tremor in his leg— although, as he said, he did not recommend the treatment. The explosion may have altered his mental capabilities as well, but for the worse.

Were there sufficient training grounds to assemble that many divisions? The reconstitution of the division groups in Russia could have taken place in the rear of the armies, reducing the time between the withdrawal of each division group and the return of the first new division. There were ample training grounds in France that had been used for four years to create divisions. The occupation divisions could have been re-formed in place.

Why did the Replacement Army not carry out this program? It was delayed, as we have seen, because the conspirators wanted a large trained force available to control Germany after Hitler was killed. The program was planned and carried out later in August and September 1944 with the creation of the *Volksgrenadier* divisions.

All of the divisions would have been infantry; what about panzer divisions? Although the Germans could have used additional panzer divisions in Russia, there was an adequate number in France. Tank production had been utilized to rebuild panzer divisions in France from November 1943 to June 1944. That more could have been done is doubtful. The real problem in both East and West was the lack of infantry divisions to defend positions, not panzer divisions to launch attacks.

Whatever other questions there may be concerning the creation of a strategic reserve before June 1944, the lack of such a reserve resulted in two disasters in the summer of 1944. Despite a crash program in August and September to replace the lost divisions, and spoiling offensives in Belgium and in Hungary later in the year, the German cause on those fronts was on a downward spiral.

In the East, the German cause was likewise doomed. In White Russia the Red Army had inflicted a staggering defeat on the German army. Not only did the Germans suffer heavy losses in manpower, but the nature of the battle—multiple pockets created and destroyed by the Russians—resulted in heavy losses in equipment and the destruction of entire divisions. In June alone, twenty-five divisions (twenty-one infantry, one panzer, one panzer grenadier, and two air force divisions) were destroyed. Another twenty-eight German divisions were destroyed in July. The loss of these German divisions came at a crucial period, when a similar annihilation of German forces was occurring in France. Therefore, there were no reserves available, except a few divisions in Norway and the Balkans.

The battle for White Russia helped bring the war to a close but also opened the way for the Soviet Union's domination of Eastern Europe. The Western Allies' request to Stalin to start a diversion in the East in June 1944 to dilute German attention and strength in the West during the invasion of France was all too effective; it gave the Soviet Union an incentive to march into Poland, the gateway to the West, and occupy more of Europe than anyone had dreamed. The mighty bear had been unleashed, and only many decades later would it be bridled again.

The Western Allies needed Soviet help to stop the dreaded Wehrmacht before Hitler could develop weapons of mass destruction, as well as to save thousands of British and American lives. The die was cast long before Yalta. Roosevelt and Churchill did not hand over Eastern Europe on a silver platter; the Red Army grabbed the platter, with hard-fought battles. The victories were won with Soviet lives and weapons and with a significant amount of Lead-Lease assistance. At the end of hostilities, the Russian bear did not return to its cage like a docile circus performer but retained control of the countries that it had liberated from German oppression. The lines drawn at Yalta only reflected the antici-pated situation at the end of the war and applied an age-old principle— you keep what you possess when the war ends. The Soviet strangle hold on Eastern Europe would remain until the end of the Cold War over forty years later.

Bibliography

Babich, P., and A.G. Baier. *Razvitie Vooruzheniia i Organizatsii Sovetski Suxoputnikh Voisk v Godi Velikoi Otechestvennoi Voini.* Moscow: Izdanie Akademii, 1990.

Bartov, Omer. *Hitler's Army: Soldiers, Nazis, and War in the Third Reich.* New York: Oxford University Press, 1991.

Bender, Roger J., and Hugh P. Taylor. *Uniforms, Oranization and History of the Waffen SS.* 4 vols. Mountain View, Calif.: Bender, 1971–76.

Brown, Anthony. *Bodyguard of Lies.* New York: Harper and Row, 1975.

Bryant, Arthur. *The Turn of the Tide.* Garden City, N.Y.: Doubleday, 1957.

Carell, Paul. *Invasion: They're Coming.* New York: Bantam, 1964.

Chuikov, V.I. *The End of the Third Reich.* Moscow: Progress, 1978.

Churchill, Winston S. *Closing the Ring.* Vol. 5 of *The Second World War.* Boston: Houghton Mifflin, 1951.

Dunn, Walter S., Jr. *Hitler's Nemesis: The Red Army, 1930–1945.* Westport, Conn.: Praeger, 1994.

———. Kursk: *Hitler's Gamble, 1943.* Westport, Conn.: Praeger, 1997.

———. *Second Front Now, 1943.* Tuscaloosa, Ala.: University of Alabama Press, 1981.

———. *Soviet Blitzkrieg: The Battle for White Russia, 1944.* Boulder, Colo.: Lynne Rienner, 2000.

Erickson, John. *The Road to Berlin.* Boulder, Colo.: Westview Press, 1983.

Fremde Heer Ost. Captured German Records. National Archives. *Geschichte des Grossen Vaterlandischen Krieges der Sowjetunion.* 8 vols. Berlin: Deutscher Militarverlag, 1964.

Glantz, David M. *Art of War Symposium. From the Dnepr to the Vistula: Soviet Offensive Operations, November 1943–August 1944.* Carlisle Barracks, Pa.: U.S. Army War College, 1985.

Glantz, David M., and Jonathan M. House. *When Titans Clashed: How the Red Army Stopped Hitler.* Lawrence: University Press of Kansas, 1995.

Glantz, David M., and Harold S. Orenstein, eds. *Belorussia 1944: The Soviet General Staff Study.* Carlisle, Pa.: David M. Glantz, 1998.

Goebbels, Josef P. *The Goebbels Diaries, 1942–1943.* Edited by Louis P. Lochner. New York: Universal-Award House, 1971.

Gray, Carl R. *Railroading in Eighteen Countries.* New York: Scribner's, 1955

Great Britain. War Office. *German Order of Battle, 1944.* London: Hippocrene, 1975.

Harrison, Gordon. *Cross Channel Attack: United States Army in World War II.* Washington, D.C.: Department of the Army, 1951.

Haupt, Werner von. *Die 260. Infanterie-Division, 1939–1944.* Bad Nauheim and Dorheim: Verlag Hans-Henning Podzun, 1970.

———.*Geschichte der 134. Infanterie Division.* Weinsberg: Herausgegeben vom Kamardenkreis der Ehemaligen, 134, Inf.-Division, 1971.

Keilig, Wolf. *Das Deutsche Heer, 1939–1945.* 3 vols. Bad Nauheim: Podzun, 1956–72.

Klink, Ernst. *Das Gesetz des Handelns die Operation "Zitadelle," 1943.* Stuttgart: Deutsche Verlags-Anstalt, 1966.

Koltunov, G.A. *Kurskaia Bitva.* Moscow: Voenizdat, 1970.

Krivosheev, G.F. *Grif Sekretnosti Snyat: Poteri Vooruzhenikh sil SSSR v Voinakh Voevikh Deistviiakh i Voennikh Konflitakh.* Moscow: Izdatelstvo, 1993.

Lucas, James. *War on the Eastern Front 1941–1945: The German Soldier in Russia.* New York: Bonanza Books, 1979.

Manstein, Erich von. *Lost Victories.* Novato, Calif.: Presidio Press, 1982.

Mehner, Kurt, ed. *Die Geheimentages Berichte der Deutschen Wermacht-fuhrung im Zweiten Weltkrieg 1939–1945.* Vol. 7. Osnabruck: Biblio Verlag, 1988.

Mueller-Hillebrand, Burkhart. *Das Heer, 1933–1945.* 3 vols. Frankfurt am Main: E.S. Mittler and Sohn, 1959–69.

Niepold, G. *The Battle for White Russia: The Destruction of Army Group Centre, June 1944.* London: Brassey's, 1987.

Parotkin, Ivan, ed. *The Battle of Kursk.* Moscow: Progress, 1974.

Pogue, Forrest C. *Ordeal and Hope.* Vol. 2 of *George C. Marshall.* New York: Viking, 1967.

———. *Organizer of Victory.* Vol. 3 of *George C. Marshall.* New York: Viking, 1973.

Records of German Field Commands, Divisions, Sixty-fifth Division, Captured German Records, Microfilm Series GG 65, T315, roll 1037.

Sajer, Guy. *The Forgotten Soldier.* New York: Harper and Row, 1971.

Schramm, Percy Ernst. *Kriegstagebuch des Oberkommandos der Wehrmacht.* 4 vols. Frankfurt am Main: Bernard und Graefe, 1961–65.

Seaton, Albert. *The Russo-German War, 1941–1945.* New York: Praeger, 1970.

Shulman, Milton. *Defeat in the West.* New York: Dutton, 1948.

Speer, Albert. *Inside the Third Reich.* New York: Macmillan, 1970.

Stoler, Mark A. *The Politics of the Second Front.* Westport, Conn.: Greenwood Press, 1977.

Tessin, Georg. *Verbande und Truppen der Deutschen Wehmacht und Waffen SS in Zweiten Weltkrieg, 1939–1945.* 14 vols. Osnabruck: Biblio Verlag, 1965–80.

United States. War Department. *Handbook of German Military Forces. Technical Manual: Enemy 30-451.* Washington, D.C.: Government Printing Office, 1945.

Warlimont, Walter. *Inside Hitler's Headquarters, 1939–1945.* New York: Praeger, 1964.

Wedemeyer, Albert C. *Wedemeyer Reports!* New York: Henry Holt, 1958.

Westphal, Siegfried. *The German Army in the West.* London: Cassell, 1951.

Winterbotham, Fred W. *The Ultra Secret.* New York: Dell, 1974.

Ziemke, Earl F. *Stalingrad to Berlin: The German Campaign in Russia, 1942–1945.* New York: Dorset Press, 1968.

Index

Aachen, 80
Afrika Korps, 4
alarm units, xv, 16, 20, 38
Allenstein, 82
Arnhem, 8
Antwerp, 21
Anzio, 71
Aschaffenburg, 85
Augsburg, 83

Baden-Baden, 85
Balkans, 1, 16, 18, 31, 35, 38, 44, 53, 59, 72–73, 78
Baumholder, 94
Belgium, 48
Berlin, xviii, 66
Bielefeld, 80, 85
Birley, Eric, viii, 157
Bischofsburg, 85
Blau, 16

Bobruysk, 137, 139–146, 148–149, 150–151
Bogushevsk, 114, 125–127, 129–130
Bohm, 83
Bonn, 85
Braunschweig, 85
Busch, Ernest, 117, 119, 125, 129, 143–144

Calais, 89
Camp Arys, 17
Camp Bitsch, 20
Camp Kilmer, NJ, 5
Casablanca, 24
Caumont, 101
Cherbourg, 102
Churchill, Winston, viii, 50–51, 89, 91, 167
Cologne, 80

About the Author

WALTER S. DUNN JR. is an independent writer and researcher. He had a 40-year career directing museums, including the Buffalo & Erie County Historical Society and the Iowa Science Center. He received a Ph.D. from the University of Wisconsin, Madison. His latest book is *Opening New Markets: The British Army and the American Frontier, 1764–1768* (2002).